Finest Recipe
Collection

Finest Recipe Collection

PUBLICATIONS INTERNATIONAL, LTD.

Pictured on front cover: Spring Fling Fruit Tart *(page 154).*

Pictured on back cover *(clockwise from top):* Napoleons *(page 174)*, Almond Cheesecake with Raspberries *(page 202),* Swordfish with Leek Cream *(page 150)* and Seafood Ravioli with Fresh Tomato Sauce *(page 38).*

Library of Congress Catalog Card Number:

ISBN: 1-56173-547-7

This edition published by Publications International, Ltd., 7373 North Cicero Avenue, Lincolnwood, IL 60646.

Manufactured in U.S.A.

8   7   6   5   4   3   2   1

Contents

A Word About *PHILLY*

PHILADELPHIA BRAND Cream Cheese Products... for the way we live today.

American moms and other great chefs have been baking, cooking and entertaining with PHILADELPHIA BRAND Cream Cheese for generations and PHILLY Cream Cheese is still America's favorite! It's the perfect ingredient for a variety of foods from appetizers and side dishes to main meal fare and desserts. PHILLY Cream Cheese products add a real touch of elegance to even the simplest of recipes.

The versatility of PHILLY Cream Cheese products makes them a natural for today's cooking. The smooth creamy texture can be spread, blended, melted, baked, cooked or simply topped on your favorite dish. And today you'll find PHILLY Cream Cheese products in a variety of convenient forms to fit all your needs. You know that PHILADELPHIA BRAND Cream Cheese brick has always been ideal for baking and cooking. But did you know that you can substitute Light PHILADELPHIA BRAND Neufchatel Cheese brick in your recipes and still get that creamy delicious taste with 33% less fat?

Although it was developed to be and is most often used as a spreading cheese, PHILADELPHIA BRAND Soft Cream Cheese is suitable for many recipes. You'll especially like the easy blending qualities of PHILLY Cream Cheese when preparing quick chilled recipes such as dips, spreads, frostings, cold sauces or fillings. In recipes calling for brick cream cheese, soft cream cheese should not be substituted because a softer consistency may result.

Whatever the occasion, PHILLY Cream Cheese products help make the most of it!

7

40 Fabulous Appetizers

HOT CHEESY ALMOND SPREAD

You may want to double the recipe for any appetizer party... this favorite disappears rapidly!

1 (8 oz.) pkg. PHILADELPHIA
    BRAND Cream Cheese, softened
1½ cups (6 ozs.) KRAFT Shredded Swiss
    Cheese
⅓ cup KRAFT Real Mayonnaise
¼ cup chopped green onion
⅛ teaspoon ground nutmeg
⅛ teaspoon pepper
¼ cup sliced almonds, toasted

- Preheat oven to 350°.
- Beat all ingredients except almonds in small mixing bowl at medium speed with electric mixer until well blended. Stir in almonds. Spread into 9-inch pie plate.
- Bake 15 minutes, stirring after 8 minutes. Serve with assorted crackers or party rye bread slices. *2⅓ cups*

Prep time: 15 minutes
Cooking time: 15 minutes

MICROWAVE: • Prepare recipe as directed except for baking. • Microwave on MEDIUM (50%) 6 minutes or until Swiss cheese is melted and mixture is warm, stirring after 4 minutes. (*Do not overcook.*) • Stir before serving. Garnish with additional toasted sliced almonds, if desired. Serve with assorted crackers or party rye bread slices.

Microwave cooking time: 6 minutes

SHRIMP AND CHINESE PEA PODS

This unique dip is a zesty blend of PHILLY Cream Cheese, watercress, mayonnaise and lemon juice.

1½ cups packed watercress leaves
1 (8 oz.) pkg. PHILADELPHIA
    BRAND Cream Cheese, softened
¼ cup KRAFT Real Mayonnaise
¼ cup green onion slices
1½ tablespoons lemon juice
¼ teaspoon salt
1½ lbs. medium shrimp, cleaned, cooked
½ lb. pea pods, blanched
1 red pepper, cut into thin strips
1 leek, cut into thin strips

- Place all ingredients except shrimp, pea pods, peppers and leek in food processor or blender container; process until well blended. Chill.
- Wrap shrimp with pea pod; garnish with peppers. Tie knot with leek to secure. Serve with watercress dip.
Approximately 3 dozen

Prep time: 45 minutes plus chilling

Tip: Omit leek and pepper strips. Secure with wooden picks.

◆◆◆

Shell and devein shrimp before cooking. To cook 1 pound of shrimp, combine 1 cup cold water, 1 cup dry white wine, 2 to 3 peppercorns, 1 bay leaf and 3 to 4 lemon slices in large saucepan; bring to boil. Add shrimp; reduce heat and simmer 3 to 5 minutes or until shrimp turn pink. Drain. Chill.

9

Shrimp and Chinese Pea Pods

SPINACH–CHEESE BOREK

1 (8 oz.) container PHILADELPHIA
  BRAND Soft Cream Cheese with
  Chives & Onion
1 (10 oz.) pkg. BIRDS EYE Chopped
  Spinach, thawed, well drained
⅓ cup roasted red peppers, drained,
  chopped
⅛ teaspoon black pepper
9 frozen phyllo sheets, thawed
6 tablespoons PARKAY Margarine,
  melted

- Preheat oven to 375°.
- Stir together cream cheese, spinach, red
  peppers and black pepper in medium
  bowl until well blended.
- Lay one sheet phyllo dough on flat
  surface. Brush with margarine; cut
  lengthwise into four 18×3½-inch strips.
- For each appetizer, spoon about
  1 tablespoon filling onto dough about
  1 inch from one end of each strip. Fold the
  end over filling at 45° angle. Continue
  folding as you would fold a flag to form a
  triangle that encloses filling. Repeat with
  remaining phyllo and filling.
- Place triangles on greased cookie sheet.
  Brush with margarine.
- Bake 12 to 15 minutes or until golden
  brown.   *3 dozen*

Prep time: 30 minutes
Cooking time: 15 minutes

Note: Before making final fold of triangle,
place small herb sprig on phyllo. Fold dough
over herb (herb will be on top of appetizer).
Bake as directed.

◆ ◆ ◆

*Thaw phyllo sheets in refrigerator 8 to
12 hours before using. Because phyllo
sheets dry out very quickly, have filling
prepared before removing sheets from
refrigerator. For best results, work
quickly and cover unused phyllo sheets
with damp cloth to prevent them from
drying out.*

CREAMY ITALIAN GARLIC SPREAD

1 (12 oz.) container PHILADELPHIA
  BRAND Soft Cream Cheese
¼ cup PARKAY Margarine
3 garlic cloves, minced
2 tablespoons dry white wine
1½ tablespoons chopped fresh parsley
1 tablespoon finely chopped fresh
  thyme or ½ teaspoon dried thyme
  leaves, crushed
1 tablespoon finely chopped fresh basil
  or ½ teaspoon dried basil leaves,
  crushed
Dash of salt and pepper

- Beat cream cheese, margarine and garlic
  in small mixing bowl at medium speed
  with electric mixer until well blended.
- Blend in remaining ingredients. Chill
  several hours or overnight. Serve with
  French bread slices, toasted pita wedges or
  bagel chips.   *2 cups*

Prep time: 15 minutes plus chilling

◆ ◆ ◆

*Fresh herbs create a new flavor sensation
in foods. They add personality and
dimension to a dish. PHILADELPHIA
BRAND Cream Cheese is a delicious way
to familiarize yourself with the flavor of
fresh herbs. When using fresh herbs in
place of dried, use 1 tablespoon fresh for
every ½ teaspoon crushed herbs. Let the
herb-cheese mixture stand at least 1 hour
for flavors to blend.*

Spinach-Cheese Borek

SOUTHWESTERN CHEESECAKE

All of your favorite southwestern ingredients in a savory cheesecake… fantastic looking and tasting!

   1 cup finely crushed tortilla chips
   3 tablespoons PARKAY Margarine, melted
   2 (8 oz.) pkgs. PHILADELPHIA BRAND Cream Cheese, softened
   2 eggs
   1 (8 oz.) pkg. KRAFT Shredded Colby/ Monterey Jack Cheese
   1 (4 oz.) can chopped green chilies, drained
   1 cup BREAKSTONE'S Sour Cream
   1 cup chopped orange or yellow pepper
   ½ cup green onion slices
   ⅓ cup chopped tomatoes
   ¼ cup pitted ripe olive slices

• Preheat oven to 325°.
• Stir together chips and margarine in small bowl; press onto bottom of 9-inch springform pan. Bake 15 minutes.
• Beat cream cheese and eggs in large mixing bowl at medium speed with electric mixer until well blended. Mix in shredded cheese and chilies; pour over crust. Bake 30 minutes.
• Spread sour cream over cheesecake. Loosen cake from rim of pan; cool before removing rim of pan. Chill.
• Top with remaining ingredients just before serving.   *16 to 20 servings*

Prep time: 20 minutes plus chilling
Cooking time: 30 minutes

◆ ◆ ◆

To make an attractive design on top of this cheesecake, simply cut three diamonds out of paper. Place on top of cheesecake. Place green onion slices around diamonds. Remove cutouts; fill in with peppers. Add a strip of tomatoes down the center. Garnish with olives.

COCONUT CHEESE SPREAD

A delicious spread to keep on hand, ready in an instant for guests or as a quick snack.

   1 (8 oz.) container PHILADELPHIA BRAND Soft Cream Cheese with Pineapple
   ½ cup BAKER'S ANGEL FLAKE Coconut
   ¼ cup macadamia nuts, coarsely chopped
   ½ teaspoon ground ginger

• Stir together ingredients in small bowl until well blended. Serve with apple slices and date nut or brown bread slices.
                                      1 cup

Prep time: 10 minutes

12

13

SPICY COEUR À LA CRÈME

A variation on a classic French delicacy, this appetizer will add pizzazz to any party.

   3 (8 oz.) pkgs. PHILADELPHIA
      BRAND Cream Cheese, softened
   ½ cup chopped green onion
   2 tablespoons chopped fresh cilantro
      (optional)
   2 garlic cloves, minced
   1 teaspoon ground cumin
   ½ teaspoon salt
      Dash of cayenne pepper (optional)
   ⅓ cup salsa

- Place all ingredients except salsa in food processor or blender container; process until well blended.
- Line coeur à la crème or 3-cup mold with cheesecloth or plastic wrap. Pour in cream cheese mixture. Cover with cheesecloth or plastic wrap. Chill several hours or overnight.
- Unwrap top of mold. Unmold; carefully remove cheesecloth or plastic wrap.
- Top with salsa. Garnish with sprig of cilantro, if desired. Serve with tortilla chips.   *Approximately 2½ cups*

Prep time: 20 minutes plus chilling

DIJON HERB DIP

There's no need to limit yourself to serving this dip with just artichokes—this herb dip is delicious with any vegetable dipper.

   1 (8 oz.) pkg. Light PHILADELPHIA
      BRAND Neufchatel Cheese,
      softened
   3 tablespoons plain yogurt
   2 tablespoons KRAFT 100% Grated
      Parmesan Cheese
   2 teaspoons Dijon mustard
   1 teaspoon white wine worcestershire
      sauce
   ½ teaspoon dried chervil (optional)

- Place ingredients in food processor or blender container; process until well blended.
- Serve with cooked artichokes. Garnish with lemon wedges, if desired.   *1 cup*

Prep time: 10 minutes

To prepare artichokes, wash artichokes and cut off stems at bases. Remove tough outer leaves. Cut off top thirds of artichokes; trim prickly leaf tips. To prevent discoloration during cooking, rub artichokes with lemon juice before cooking. Stand artichokes upright in saucepan. Add enough boiling water to completely cover artichokes. Add about 1 teaspoon salt to water. Cover; cook 40 minutes, or until a leaf pulls out easily. Drain.

14

Dijon Herb Dip

ORIENTAL SPREAD

 1 (12 oz.) container PHILADELPHIA
    BRAND Soft Cream Cheese
⅔ cup shredded carrots
½ cup chopped salted peanuts
¼ cup chopped water chestnuts
¼ cup green onion slices
 2 tablespoons soy sauce
 1 tablespoon chopped fresh cilantro
 1 small garlic clove, minced
¼ teaspoon ground ginger
 2 tablespoons sweet and sour sauce

• Spread cream cheese onto bottom of
  10-inch serving plate.
• Mix together all remaining ingredients
  except sweet and sour sauce in medium
  bowl. Spoon vegetable mixture evenly
  over cream cheese mixture to within
  ½ inch from edge. Drizzle with sauce.
  Serve with crackers.   *12 to 14 servings*

Prep time: 20 minutes

BACKYARD BRUNCH CITRUS DIP

*Add interest to these fruit kabob dippers
by cutting fruit into geometric shapes
before skewering.*

 1 (8 oz.) pkg. Light PHILADELPHIA
    BRAND Neufchatel Cheese,
    softened
½ cup frozen orange juice concentrate,
    thawed
 2 tablespoons skim milk

• Place ingredients in food processor or
  blender container; process until well
  blended. Chill. Serve with assorted fruit
  dippers.   *1½ cups*

Prep time: 5 minutes plus chilling

SUMMER SALMON TERRINE

*A light appetizer certain to impress your
guests.*

 1 envelope unflavored gelatin
¼ cup cold water
 1 cup BREAKSTONE'S LIGHT
    CHOICE Sour Half and Half
 1 (8 oz.) container PHILADELPHIA
    BRAND Soft Cream Cheese with
    Smoked Salmon
 2 (7½ oz.) cans salmon, drained,
    boned, flaked
 2 teaspoons lemon juice
 1 cup shredded peeled cucumber, well
    drained
½ teaspoon dried dill weed
½ teaspoon salt

• Soften gelatin in water in small saucepan;
  stir over low heat until dissolved. Stir in
  sour half and half.
• Beat cream cheese, salmon and lemon
  juice in large mixing bowl at medium
  speed with electric mixer until well
  blended. Stir in half of gelatin mixture.
• Spread half of salmon mixture onto
  bottom of lightly oiled 9×5-inch loaf pan.
• Add cucumber and seasonings to
  remaining gelatin mixture in small bowl;
  mix well. Spoon over salmon layer.
• Top with remaining salmon mixture. Chill
  until firm. Unmold.
• Serve each slice on a bed of thinly sliced
  cucumbers. Garnish with red pepper
  strips and fresh dill sprig, if desired.
                              8 servings

Prep time: 35 minutes plus chilling

◆ ◆ ◆

*For more decorative cucumbers, firmly
pull tines of fork lengthwise down cucumber. Repeat on all sides of cucumber.*

Summer Salmon Terrine

NUTTY TROPICAL SPREAD

2 (8 oz.) containers PHILADELPHIA BRAND Soft Cream Cheese with Pineapple
½ cup chopped macadamia nuts
½ cup BAKER'S ANGEL FLAKE Coconut
2 tablespoons packed brown sugar
1 tablespoon PARKAY Margarine

• Spread cream cheese onto bottom of 9-inch pie plate.
• Mix together remaining ingredients in small bowl until crumbly. Sprinkle over cream cheese.
• Broil 1 to 2 minutes or until topping is bubbly. Serve warm with fresh fruit.

12 to 15 servings

Prep time: 10 minutes
Cooking time: 2 minutes

CLASSIC DIP

1 (8 oz.) container PHILADELPHIA BRAND Soft Cream Cheese
1 (0.6 oz.) envelope GOOD SEASONS Zesty Italian Salad Dressing Mix
1 (8 oz.) container plain yogurt
1 tablespoon milk

• Stir together ingredients in small bowl until well blended. Chill. Serve with assorted vegetable dippers.   *1 cup*

Prep time: 10 minutes plus chilling

HERBED CUCUMBER CANAPÉS

Quick, easy and attractive . . . the essential elements of weekday entertaining. This PHILLY Cream Cheese spread can be prepared in advance and chilled until ready to serve.

1 (8 oz.) pkg. PHILADELPHIA BRAND Cream Cheese, softened
2 garlic cloves, minced
½ cup green onion slices
½ cup chopped fresh parsley
½ teaspoon dried thyme leaves, crushed
½ teaspoon salt
¼ teaspoon pepper
¼ teaspoon dried tarragon leaves, crushed
1 English or European cucumber, cut into ⅛- to ¼-inch slices

• Beat all ingredients except cucumber in large mixing bowl at medium speed with electric mixer until well blended.
• Spread cucumber slices with cream cheese mixture. Garnish with assorted vegetables and fresh herbs, if desired.

Approximately 3½ dozen

Prep time: 20 minutes

Variation: Substitute Light PHILADELPHIA BRAND Neufchatel Cheese for cream cheese.

◆ ◆ ◆

European cucumbers are longer than ordinary cucumbers. They are seedless and require no peeling.

Herbed Cucumber Canapés

PUMPKIN SEED DIP

1 (8 oz.) pkg. Light PHILADELPHIA
    BRAND Neufchatel Cheese,
    softened
1 cup BREAKSTONE'S LIGHT
    CHOICE Sour Half and Half
2 tablespoons milk
1 (4 oz.) can chopped green chilies,
    drained
⅓ cup hulled pumpkin seeds, toasted,
    crumbled
2 tablespoons finely chopped fresh
    cilantro
1 tablespoon finely chopped green
    onion
½ teaspoon garlic salt
¼ to ½ teaspoon hot pepper sauce

- Beat neufchatel cheese, sour half and half
  and milk in small mixing bowl at medium
  speed with electric mixer until well
  blended.
- Stir in remaining ingredients. Chill. Serve
  with jicama, celery and carrot sticks.

2⅔ cups

Prep time: 20 minutes plus chilling

---◆◆◆---

*Pumpkin seeds, commonly referred to as
pepitas or squash seeds, can be found in
most health food stores.*

*Hulled pumpkin seeds puff slightly and
become light and fragile when toasted,
making the seeds easy to crumble.*

BLACK BEAN SPIRALS

*Guests will think you have fussed for
hours making these easy Mexican
appetizers.*

4 ozs. PHILADELPHIA BRAND Cream
    Cheese, softened
½ cup (2 ozs.) KRAFT Shredded
    Monterey Jack Cheese with
    Jalapeño Peppers
¼ cup BREAKSTONE'S Sour Cream
¼ teaspoon onion salt
1 cup canned black beans, rinsed,
    drained
3 (10-inch) flour tortillas

- Beat cheeses, sour cream and onion salt
  in small mixing bowl at medium speed
  with electric mixer until well blended.
- Place beans in food processor or blender
  container; process until smooth. Spread
  thin layer of beans onto each tortilla;
  spread cheese mixture over beans.
- Roll tortillas up tightly; chill 30 minutes.
  Cut into ½-inch slices. Serve with salsa.

12 servings

Prep time: 15 minutes plus chilling

---◆◆◆---

*Black beans are grown in southern, Gulf
Coastal and Yucatan Mexico. Black beans
are high in fiber, protein, iron and potas-
sium and low in sodium.*

Black Bean Spirals

CREAMY HERB FONDUE

2 tablespoons minced shallots
1 tablespoon PARKAY Margarine
2 tablespoons dry vermouth
1 (8 oz.) container PHILADELPHIA
    BRAND Soft Cream Cheese with
    Herb & Garlic
¼ cup half and half

- Sauté shallots in margarine in medium saucepan until tender. Add vermouth; cook over low heat 1 minute.
- Stir in cream cheese and half and half; cook until cream cheese is melted. Serve warm with large cooked shrimp and sourdough bread cubes.   *1¼ cups*

Prep time: 5 minutes
Cooking time: 5 minutes

CHILLED MELON SOUP

With melons so plentiful in the summer, make double batches of this flavorful soup and store in the refrigerator for quick enjoyment.

1 (8 oz.) container PHILADELPHIA
    BRAND Soft Cream Cheese with
    Pineapple
2 cups cantaloupe chunks
1 cup honeydew melon chunks
1 cup orange juice
¼ teaspoon salt

- Place ingredients in food processor or blender container; process until well blended. Chill.   *4 servings*

Prep time: 10 minutes plus chilling

GARDEN GREEK APPETIZER

The PHILLY Cream Cheese base for this attractive appetizer can be prepared several days in advance, covered tightly and chilled. Near serving time, add the colorful fresh vegetables and arrange the crackers around the edge.

1 (8 oz.) pkg. Light PHILADELPHIA
    BRAND Neufchatel Cheese,
    softened
1 (8 oz.) pkg. CHURNY ATHENOS
    Feta Cheese, crumbled
2 tablespoons plain yogurt
1 tablespoon packed chopped fresh
    mint leaves or ½ teaspoon dried
    mint leaves, crushed
1 garlic clove, minced
1 tomato, seeded, diced
1 small cucumber, diced
1 green onion, sliced

- Beat cheeses, yogurt, mint and garlic in small mixing bowl at medium speed with electric mixer until well blended. Spread into 10-inch tart pan or pie plate. Chill.
- Top cheese mixture with tomatoes, cucumbers and onions just before serving. Serve with crackers or toasted pita bread wedges.   *10 to 12 servings*

Prep time: 15 minutes plus chilling

22

Garden Greek Appetiser

QUICK POTATO LATKES WITH SALMON SAUCE

**3 cups frozen Southern-style hash
  brown potatoes, thawed, well
  drained
2 eggs, beaten
1 small onion, quartered
¼ cup flour
¼ teaspoon CALUMET Baking Powder
¼ teaspoon salt
  Oil
  Salmon Sauce**

- Place potatoes, eggs, onions, flour, baking powder and salt in food processor container; process until potatoes and onions are finely chopped.
- Spoon level measuring tablespoonfuls potato mixture into 1½ inches hot oil. Fry until golden brown, turning once. Keep warm in oven.
- Repeat with remaining potato mixture. Serve with Salmon Sauce.   *2½ dozen*

SALMON SAUCE

**1 (8 oz.) container PHILADELPHIA
  BRAND Soft Cream Cheese with
  Smoked Salmon
½ cup BREAKSTONE'S Sour Cream
¼ cup KRAFT Real Mayonnaise
½ teaspoon chopped fresh dill**

- Stir together all ingredients in small bowl until well blended.

Prep time: 20 minutes
Cooking time: 15 minutes

PEPPERONCINI SPREAD

It's best to make this spread early in the day or even the day before your party so flavors can blend.

**1 (8 oz.) container PHILADELPHIA
  BRAND Soft Cream Cheese
½ cup (2 ozs.) shredded provolone
  cheese
¼ cup (1 oz.) KRAFT 100% Grated
  Parmesan Cheese
⅛ teaspoon garlic powder
1 (12 oz.) jar pepperoncini, drained,
  stemmed, seeded, chopped
1 plum tomato, diced**

- Stir together cheeses and garlic powder in medium bowl until well blended.
- Add pepperoncini and tomatoes; mix well. Chill. Garnish with fresh chives and green, red and yellow pepper cutouts, if desired. Serve with toasted bread cutouts.
  2½ cups

Prep time: 20 minutes plus chilling

◆◆◆

Cut bread slices with 2-inch cookie cutters. Bake at 325°, 5 minutes per side or until lightly toasted on both sides.

24

Pepperoncini Spread

OLÉ SPINACH DIP

Host an international buffet with appetizers from around the world. This creamy spinach dip is a natural accompaniment to other PHILLY Cream Cheese recipes such as Pepperoncini Spread, Spinach-Cheese Borek and Nutty Tropical Spread, to name just a few.

1 (8 oz.) container PHILADELPHIA BRAND Soft Cream Cheese
¼ cup half and half
2 cups (8 ozs.) shredded CASINO Natural Monterey Jack Cheese with Jalapeño Peppers
1 (10 oz.) pkg. BIRDS EYE Chopped Spinach, thawed, well drained
½ cup chopped onion
½ cup chopped pitted ripe olives
1 tablespoon red wine vinegar
¼ teaspoon hot pepper sauce (optional)

- Preheat oven to 400°.
- Stir together cream cheese and half and half in medium bowl until well blended. Add remaining ingredients; mix well. Spread into 9-inch pie plate.
- Bake 20 to 25 minutes or until light golden brown. Serve with tortilla chips.

10 to 12 servings

Prep time: 15 minutes
Cooking time: 25 minutes

TORTA CALIFORNIA

This festive molded appetizer features a savory blend of PHILLY Cream Cheese, goat cheese and thyme, layered with bright green pesto and roasted red peppers.

2 (8 oz.) pkgs. PHILADELPHIA BRAND Cream Cheese, softened
1 (8 oz.) pkg. goat cheese
1 to 2 garlic cloves
2 tablespoons olive oil
1 teaspoon dried thyme leaves
3 tablespoons pesto, well drained
⅓ cup roasted red peppers, drained, chopped

- Line 1-quart soufflé dish or loaf pan with plastic wrap.
- Place cream cheese, goat cheese and garlic in food processor or blender container; process until well blended. Add oil and thyme; blend well.
- Place one third of cheese mixture in soufflé dish; cover with pesto, half of remaining cheese mixture and peppers. Top with remaining cheese mixture. Cover; chill.
- Unmold; remove plastic wrap. Smooth sides. Garnish with fresh herbs and additional red peppers, if desired. Serve with assorted crackers or French bread.

3 cups

Prep time: 15 minutes plus chilling

26

Torta California

ROASTED GARLIC DIP

2 heads (4 ozs.) garlic
1 (8 oz.) pkg. PHILADELPHIA
BRAND Cream Cheese, softened
¼ cup chopped roasted red peppers
2 tablespoons dry Marsala wine
2 tablespoons olive oil
¼ teaspoon salt
⅛ teaspoon white pepper

- Preheat oven to 350°.
- Remove outer papery skin from both heads of garlic, leaving heads intact; place in small baking dish. Add water to dish to 1-inch depth; cover with foil.
- Bake 1 hour or until garlic is tender, basting occasionally with water.
- Remove skins from garlic cloves; place garlic in food processor or blender container. Add remaining ingredients; process until smooth. Chill. Garnish with chopped fresh chives and red pepper, if desired. Serve with vegetable dippers.

1½ cups

Prep time: 10 minutes plus chilling
Cooking time: 1 hour

DOUBLE CHEESE TIMBALES IN PEAR WINE SAUCE

1 tablespoon PARKAY Margarine
Dry bread crumbs
1 (8 oz.) pkg. PHILADELPHIA
BRAND Cream Cheese, softened
½ cup (2 ozs.) KRAFT Blue Cheese
Crumbles
3 tablespoons PARKAY Margarine
2 eggs
¼ teaspoon white pepper
⅛ teaspoon salt
2 egg whites
Pear Wine Sauce

- Preheat oven to 350°.
- Generously grease medium-size muffin pan with 1 tablespoon margarine. Lightly coat with bread crumbs.
- Beat cheeses and 3 tablespoons margarine in large mixing bowl at medium speed with electric mixer until well blended. Blend in whole eggs and seasonings.
- Beat egg whites in small mixing bowl at high speed with electric mixer until stiff peaks form. Fold into cream cheese mixture.
- Spoon cream cheese mixture into prepared muffin pan, filling each cup ¾ full. Place in large shallow baking pan. Place pan on oven rack; carefully pour boiling water into baking pan to ½-inch depth.
- Bake 25 minutes or until lightly browned and set in center. Unmold; serve warm with Pear Wine Sauce.

1 dozen

PEAR WINE SAUCE

1 (16 oz.) can pear halves, drained
¼ cup port wine

- Place pears in food processor or blender container; process until smooth.
- Bring wine to boil in small saucepan; reduce heat. Simmer 1 minute. Stir in pears; cook until thoroughly heated.

Prep time: 15 minutes
Cooking time: 25 minutes

Note: Timbales may be baked ahead of time, wrapped securely and frozen. To serve, place frozen timbales in circle in pie plate. Microwave on MEDIUM (50%) 2 minutes. Rotate dish ¼ turn. Microwave on MEDIUM (50%) 1 to 2 minutes or until warm.

◆◆◆

For best results, separate eggs when they are cold; allow them to come to room temperature before beating for maximum volume.

28

Roasted Garlic Dip

SPINACH BALLS

2 (10 oz.) pkgs. BIRDS EYE Chopped
    Spinach, thawed, well drained
1 (8 oz.) container PHILADELPHIA
    BRAND Soft Cream Cheese with
    Herb & Garlic
2 eggs
⅔ cup (3 ozs.) KRAFT 100% Grated
    Parmesan Cheese
½ cup dry bread crumbs

- Preheat oven to 375°.
- Stir together all ingredients in large bowl
  until well blended. Shape into 1-inch balls.
  Place in 15×10×1-inch jelly roll pan.
- Bake 15 to 20 minutes or until firm. Serve
  with heated spaghetti sauce, if desired.

Approximately 3½ dozen

Prep time: 20 minutes
Cooking time: 20 minutes

*For well-drained spinach, layer thawed
spinach between paper towels and firmly
squeeze out all excess moisture; repeat as
necessary with additional paper towels.*

CHILLED PEAR HELENE SOUP

*Guests will be impressed with the elegant
presentation of this soup—and it's so
easy to prepare.*

4 pears, peeled, cored, cubed
1 (12 oz.) can pear nectar
1 (8 oz.) container Light
    PHILADELPHIA BRAND
    Pasteurized Process Cream Cheese
    Product
½ cup champagne
1 cup raspberries

- Place pears in food processor or blender
  container; process until smooth. Add
  nectar, cream cheese product and
  champagne; process until well blended.
  Pour into medium bowl; cover. Chill.
- When ready to serve, place raspberries in
  food processor or blender container;
  process until smooth. Strain.
- Spoon soup into individual serving bowls.
  Spoon approximately 2 tablespoons
  raspberry purée at intervals onto each
  serving. Pull wooden pick through purée
  making decorative design as desired.
  Garnish with additional raspberries and
  fresh mint leaves, if desired.

6 servings

Prep time: 10 minutes plus chilling

Chilled Pear Helene Soup

COLD SUN–DRIED TOMATO & FETA TERRINE

This terrine can be made up to one day in advance.

1 envelope unflavored gelatin
2 tablespoons cold water
3 tablespoons Madeira wine or sherry
1 (8 oz.) pkg. PHILADELPHIA BRAND Cream Cheese, softened
2 ozs. CHURNY ATHENOS Crumbled Feta Cheese
½ cup BREAKSTONE'S Sour Cream
¼ cup sun-dried tomatoes in oil, drained, finely chopped
¼ cup chopped roasted red peppers
2 tablespoons finely chopped fresh parsley
1 small garlic clove, minced

- Soften gelatin in water in small saucepan. Add wine; stir over low heat until gelatin is dissolved.
- Beat cheeses in small mixing bowl at medium speed with electric mixer until well blended. Blend in sour cream.
- Add gelatin mixture and remaining ingredients to cream cheese mixture; mix well. Pour into lightly-oiled 8×4-inch loaf pan. Chill several hours or until firm.
- Unmold; cut into slices.

10 to 12 servings

Prep time: 35 minutes plus chilling

CORONADO DIP

2 (1 lb.) boneless, skinless chicken breasts, cut into 1-inch pieces
¾ cup cold water
1 (1.5 oz.) envelope taco seasoning mix
1 (8 oz.) pkg. Light PHILADELPHIA BRAND Neufchatel Cheese, softened
1 tablespoon lime juice
1 tablespoon skim milk
½ cup chopped tomato
2 tablespoons shredded KRAFT Light Naturals Reduced Fat Sharp Cheddar Cheese
2 tablespoons shredded KRAFT Light Naturals Reduced Fat Monterey Jack Cheese
2 tablespoons green onion slices
2 tablespoons chopped red pepper
1 tablespoon chopped pitted ripe olives

- Bring chicken, water and taco seasoning mix to boil in large skillet; reduce heat. Cover; simmer 25 minutes.
- Cool slightly; shred chicken.
- Place neufchatel cheese, lime juice and milk in food processor or blender container; process until well blended.
- When ready to serve, spread neufchatel cheese mixture onto center of large serving plate; surround with chicken. Top with remaining ingredients. Serve with tortilla chips. *12 servings*

Prep time: 25 minutes
Cooking time: 25 minutes

◆ ◆ ◆

To shred chicken, pull cooked chicken breasts in opposite directions using two forks. Continue until chicken is desired shred size.

32

Coronado Dip

HERB ARTICHOKE SPREAD

1 (8 oz.) container PHILADELPHIA BRAND Soft Cream Cheese with Herb & Garlic
1 (6½ oz.) jar marinated artichoke hearts, drained, chopped
¼ teaspoon salt
4 to 6 drops hot pepper sauce

• Stir together ingredients in small bowl until well blended. Chill. Serve with toasted bread cutouts. Garnish with fresh herbs and chopped red pepper, if desired.
1½ cups

Prep time: 5 minutes plus chilling

To make toasted bread cutouts, see directions page 24.

STUFFED POTATO APPETIZERS

24 small new red potatoes (approx. 1½ lbs.)
1 (8 oz.) container PHILADELPHIA BRAND Soft Cream Cheese with Herb & Garlic
¼ cup chopped fresh parsley

• Cook potatoes in boiling water in large saucepan 18 to 20 minutes or until tender. Drain; cool.
• Scoop out centers with melon baller or small pointed teaspoon, leaving ⅛-inch shell.
• Spoon or pipe cream cheese into potatoes. Sprinkle with parsley.
2 dozen

Prep time: 15 minutes
Cooking time: 20 minutes

DOUBLE RADISH DIP

Colorfully pink with flecks of red ... a nippy dip for crisp vegetables.

1 (6 oz.) bag radishes (approx. 1½ cups)
1 (8 oz.) container PHILADELPHIA BRAND Soft Cream Cheese with Chives & Onion
1 tablespoon KRAFT Prepared Horseradish
1 teaspoon worcestershire sauce

• Place radishes in food processor or blender container; process until finely chopped.
• Add remaining ingredients; process until well blended. Chill. Serve with vegetable dippers or soft bread sticks.
2 cups

Prep time: 10 minutes plus chilling

FRUITED CHEESE SPREAD

1 (8 oz.) pkg. PHILADELPHIA BRAND Cream Cheese, softened
1 (10 oz.) pkg. shredded CRACKER BARREL Muenster Cheese
½ cup finely chopped dried apricots
¼ cup finely chopped green pepper
1 tablespoon milk
⅛ to ¼ teaspoon ground ginger

• Beat ingredients in large mixing bowl at medium speed with electric mixer until well blended. Chill. Serve with assorted crackers or party rye bread slices.
2½ cups

Prep time: 15 minutes plus chilling

34

Herb Artichoke Spread

AVOCADO CRAB DIP

PHILLY Neufchatel Cheese makes this dip extra creamy.

1 large avocado, halved, pitted, peeled
2 tablespoons chopped onion
1 tablespoon lemon juice
1 teaspoon worcestershire sauce
1 (8 oz.) pkg. Light PHILADELPHIA
   BRAND Neufchatel Cheese,
   softened
½ cup BREAKSTONE'S LIGHT
   CHOICE Sour Half and Half
½ teaspoon salt
   Few drops hot pepper sauce
1 (8 oz.) pkg. LOUIS KEMP CRAB
   DELIGHTS Legs, chopped

• Place avocado, onion, lemon juice and worcestershire sauce in food processor or blender container; process until blended.
• Add neufchatel cheese, sour half and half, salt and hot pepper sauce; process until well blended. Stir in imitation crab meat. Serve with tortilla chips.   *3 cups*

Prep time: 10 minutes

REGGAE DIP WITH SHRIMP

1 to 2 garlic cloves
1 (8 oz.) container PHILADELPHIA
   BRAND Soft Cream Cheese with
   Chives & Onion
¼ cup chili sauce
2 teaspoons worcestershire sauce
1 teaspoon dry mustard
¼ teaspoon pepper
30 medium shrimp, cleaned, cooked

• Place garlic in food processor or blender container; process until finely chopped.
• Add all remaining ingredients except shrimp; process until well blended. Chill. Serve with shrimp. Garnish with lemon wedges, if desired.   *6 servings*

Prep time: 15 minutes plus chilling

PEPPERONI SPREAD

3 ozs. pepperoni
¼ cup fresh parsley, stemmed
1 (8 oz.) pkg. Light PHILADELPHIA
   BRAND Neufchatel Cheese,
   softened
3 tablespoons skim milk

• Place pepperoni and parsley in food processor or blender container; process until chopped.
• Add remaining ingredients; process until well blended. Serve with assorted vegetable dippers and bread sticks.
          1½ cups

Prep time: 10 minutes

Variation: Substitute OSCAR MAYER Smoked Cooked Ham for pepperoni.

Reggae Dip with Shrimp

SALMON CUCUMBER MOUSSE

Deliciously light and creamy, this molded mousse is an elegant buffet attraction.

2 envelopes unflavored gelatin
1 cup cold water
2 tablespoons lemon juice
2 (8 oz.) containers PHILADELPHIA BRAND Soft Cream Cheese with Smoked Salmon
1 small cucumber, peeled, finely chopped

• Soften gelatin in water in small saucepan; stir over low heat until dissolved. Stir in lemon juice.
• Stir together cream cheese, gelatin mixture and cucumber in small bowl until well blended. Pour into lightly oiled 1-quart mold.
• Chill until firm. Unmold onto serving platter. Serve with melba toast rounds.

3 cups

Prep time: 15 minutes plus chilling

SEAFOOD RAVIOLI WITH FRESH TOMATO SAUCE

PHILLY Soft Cream Cheese with Herb & Garlic combined with imitation crabmeat makes a tasty filling for these unique ravioli appetizers.

1 (8 oz.) container PHILADELPHIA BRAND Soft Cream Cheese with Herb & Garlic
¾ cup chopped LOUIS KEMP CRAB DELIGHTS Chunks, rinsed
36 wonton wrappers
   Cold water
   Fresh Tomato Sauce

• Stir together cream cheese and imitation crabmeat in medium bowl until well blended.
• For each ravioli, place 1 tablespoonful cream cheese mixture in center of one wonton wrapper. Brush edges with water. Place second wonton wrapper on top. Press edges together to seal, taking care to press out air. Repeat with remaining cream cheese mixture and wonton wrappers.
• For square-shaped ravioli, cut edges of wonton wrappers with pastry trimmer to form square. For round-shaped ravioli, place 3-inch round biscuit cutter on ravioli, making sure center of each cutter contains filling. Press down firmly, cutting through both wrappers, to trim edges. Repeat with remaining ravioli.
• Bring 1½ quarts water to boil in large saucepan. Cook ravioli, a few at a time, 2 to 3 minutes or until they rise to surface. Remove with slotted spoon. Serve hot with Fresh Tomato Sauce.

1½ dozen

FRESH TOMATO SAUCE

2 garlic cloves, minced
2 tablespoons olive oil
6 plum tomatoes, diced
1 tablespoon red wine vinegar
1 tablespoon chopped fresh parsley

• Sauté garlic in oil in medium saucepan 1 minute. Add remaining ingredients.
• Cook over low heat 2 to 3 minutes or until thoroughly heated, stirring occasionally. Cool to room temperature.

Prep time: 25 minutes
Cooking time: 3 minutes per batch

Variation: For triangle-shaped ravioli, place 2 teaspoonfuls cream cheese mixture in center of each wonton wrapper; brush edges with water. Fold in half to form triangle. Press edges together to seal, taking care to press out air. Trim edges of wonton wrapper with pastry trimmer, if desired.

3 dozen

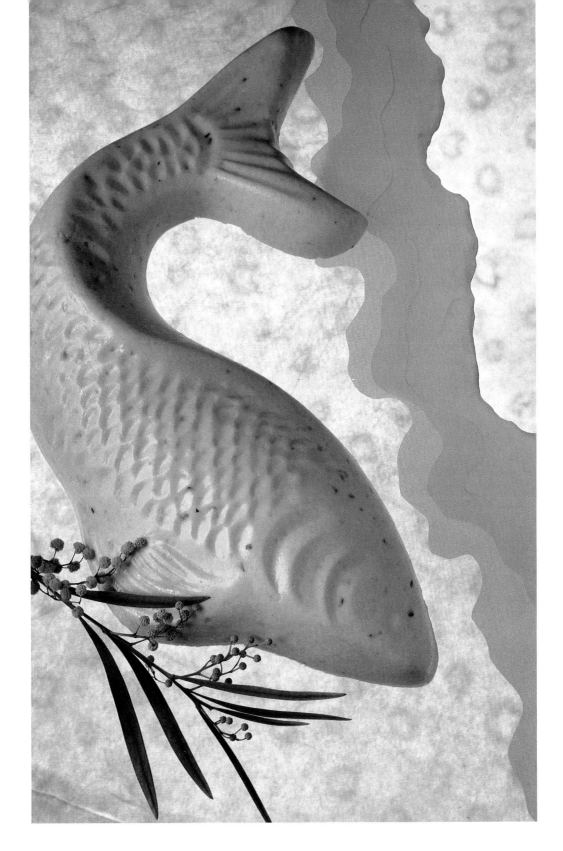

Salmon Cucumber Mousse

TURKISH CHEESE

Flaky layers of phyllo dough are baked with a creamy filling of four cheeses and seasonings for this tasty appetizer treat.

> 1 (8 oz.) pkg. PHILADELPHIA BRAND Cream Cheese, softened
> 2 eggs
> ¼ cup green onion slices
> 1 tablespoon chopped fresh dill or ½ teaspoon dried dill weed
> 1 tablespoon packed chopped fresh mint leaves or ½ teaspoon dried mint leaves, crushed
> 1 (8 oz.) pkg. CHURNY ATHENOS Feta Cheese, crumbled
> 1 cup (4 ozs.) shredded CASINO Natural Monterey Jack Cheese
> ¼ cup (1 oz.) KRAFT 100% Grated Parmesan Cheese
> 16 frozen phyllo sheets, thawed
> ¾ cup PARKAY Margarine, melted

- Preheat oven to 375°.
- Beat cream cheese, eggs, onions, dill weed and mint in small mixing bowl at medium speed with electric mixer until well blended. Stir in remaining cheeses.
- Place one sheet phyllo dough on greased 15×10×1-inch jelly roll pan; brush with margarine. Continue layering seven sheets, brushing each sheet with margarine. (Note: Dough will extend over edge of pan.)
- Spread cheese mixture over phyllo; fold edges over cheese mixture. Layer remaining phyllo sheets over cheese mixture, brushing each sheet with margarine. Tuck edges under bottom layer; drizzle with remaining margarine.
- Bake 35 to 40 minutes or until lightly browned. Cut into diamond shapes.

2 dozen

Prep time: 50 minutes
Cooking time: 40 minutes

CAVIAR–FILLED VEGETABLES

There are many flavorful alternatives to caviar... try minced clams, baby shrimp, chopped nuts, shredded carrots or chopped red pepper.

> 1 (8 oz.) container PHILADELPHIA BRAND Soft Cream Cheese
> 1 to 2 shallots, chopped
> 1 tablespoon olive oil
> ¼ teaspoon coarsely ground black pepper
> Belgian endive, radicchio or assorted vegetables
> Caviar

- Place cream cheese, shallots, oil and pepper in food processor or blender container; process until well blended.
- Spoon or pipe cream cheese mixture over vegetables; top with caviar. Garnish with orange peel or fresh herbs, if desired.

Approximately 2 dozen

Prep time: 10 minutes

40

Caviar-Filled Vegetables

Satisfying Snacks

BACON APPETIZER CRESCENTS

For extra convenience, prepare the filling in advance.

1 (8 oz.) pkg. PHILADELPHIA BRAND Cream Cheese, softened
8 OSCAR MAYER Bacon Slices, crisply cooked, crumbled
⅓ cup (1½ ozs.) KRAFT 100% Grated Parmesan Cheese
¼ cup finely chopped onion
2 tablespoons chopped fresh parsley
1 tablespoon milk
2 (8 oz.) cans refrigerated quick crescent dinner rolls
1 egg, beaten
1 teaspoon cold water

- Preheat oven to 375°.
- Beat cream cheese, bacon, parmesan cheese, onion, parsley and milk in small mixing bowl at medium speed with electric mixer until well blended.
- Separate dough into eight rectangles; firmly press perforations together to seal. Spread each rectangle with 2 rounded measuring tablespoonfuls cream cheese mixture.
- Cut each rectangle in half diagonally; repeat with opposite corners. Cut in half crosswise to form six triangles. Fold points over cream cheese mixture.
- Place on greased cookie sheet; brush with combined egg and water. Sprinkle with poppy seeds, if desired.
- Bake 12 to 15 minutes or until golden brown. Serve immediately.
                              Approximately 4 dozen

Prep time: 30 minutes
Cooking time: 15 minutes

PIZZA DIP

PHILLY Cream Cheese blended with Italian seasonings is the tasty base for this zesty dip.

1 (8 oz.) pkg PHILADELPHIA BRAND Cream Cheese, softened
1 teaspoon Italian seasoning
⅛ teaspoon garlic powder
½ cup pizza sauce
½ cup (2 ozs.) chopped pepperoni
¼ cup chopped green pepper
1 (4 oz.) can mushroom pieces and stems, drained
1 cup (4 ozs.) KRAFT Shredded Low-Moisture Part-Skim Mozzarella Cheese

- Preheat oven to 350°.
- Beat cream cheese and seasonings in small mixing bowl at medium speed with electric mixer until well blended. Spread onto bottom of 9-inch pie plate.
- Cover cream cheese mixture with pizza sauce; top with remaining ingredients.
- Bake 15 to 20 minutes or until mixture is thoroughly heated and cheese is melted. Serve with crackers.   *10 servings*

Prep time: 15 minutes
Cooking time: 20 minutes

42

43

CHILI–CHEESE SQUARES

1 (11½ oz.) can refrigerated cornbread twists
1 (8 oz.) container PHILADELPHIA BRAND Soft Cream Cheese with Chives & Onion
1 egg
½ teaspoon ground cumin
1½ cups (6 ozs.) KRAFT Shredded Colby/Monterey Jack Cheese
1 (4 oz.) can chopped green chilies, drained

- Preheat oven to 375°.
- Press cornbread dough onto bottom of greased 13×9-inch baking pan; press perforations together to seal. Bake 10 minutes.
- Stir together cream cheese, egg and cumin in medium bowl until well blended. Add cheese and chilies; mix well. Spoon over crust.
- Bake 15 minutes. Cut into squares.

2 dozen

Prep time: 10 minutes
Cooking time: 15 minutes

GARDEN VEGETABLE PLATTER

1 cup torn spinach
½ cup fresh parsley, stemmed
¼ cup cold water
3 tablespoons green onion slices
½ teaspoon dried tarragon leaves, crushed
1 (8 oz.) pkg. Light PHILADELPHIA BRAND Neufchatel Cheese, softened
¾ cup chopped cucumber
½ teaspoon lemon juice
3 drops hot pepper sauce
¼ teaspoon salt

- Bring to boil spinach, parsley, water, onions and tarragon in small saucepan. Reduce heat. Cover; simmer 1 minute. Drain.
- Place spinach mixture and all remaining ingredients in food processor or blender container; process until well blended. Chill. Serve with assorted vegetable dippers.

1½ cups

Prep time: 30 minutes plus chilling

For individual servings, tie small bundles of vegetables together with thin strips of green onion tops.

44

Garden Vegetable Platter

CROQUE PARISIENNE

This is a canapé version of the French Croque Monsieur... a toasted ham and cheese sandwich.

> 1 (12 oz.) pkg. KRAFT Shredded Sharp Cheddar Cheese
> 1 (8 oz.) pkg. PHILADELPHIA BRAND Cream Cheese, softened
> ½ cup finely chopped ham
> ½ cup green onion slices
> 2 tablespoons spicy brown mustard
> 1 French bread loaf, thinly sliced KRAFT 100% Grated Parmesan Cheese

- Beat all ingredients except bread and parmesan cheese in large mixing bowl at medium speed with electric mixer until well blended.
- Spread bread slices with cream cheese mixture; sprinkle with parmesan cheese.
- Broil until lightly browned. Serve warm.

Approximately 4 dozen

Prep time: 30 minute
Cooking time: 5 minutes

THREE–PEPPER QUESADILLAS

For extra convenience, assemble these quesadillas in advance.

> 1 cup thin green pepper strips
> 1 cup thin red pepper strips
> 1 cup thin yellow pepper strips
> ½ cup thin onion slices
> ⅓ cup PARKAY Margarine
> ½ teaspoon ground cumin
> 1 (8 oz.) pkg. PHILADELPHIA BRAND Cream Cheese, softened
> 1 (8 oz.) pkg. KRAFT Shredded Sharp Cheddar Cheese
> ½ cup (2 ozs.) KRAFT 100% Grated Parmesan Cheese
> 10 (6-inch) flour tortillas

- Preheat oven to 425°.
- Sauté peppers and onions in margarine in large skillet. Stir in cumin. Drain, reserving liquid.
- Beat cheeses in small mixing bowl at medium speed with electric mixer until well blended.
- Spoon 2 tablespoons cheese mixture onto each tortilla; top with pepper mixture. Fold tortillas in half; place on baking sheet. Brush with reserved liquid.
- Bake 10 minutes. Cut each tortilla into thirds. Serve warm with salsa.

2½ dozen

Prep time: 20 minutes
Cooking time: 10 minutes

Tip: To make ahead, prepare as directed except for baking. Cover; refrigerate. When ready to serve, bake at 425°, 15 to 20 minutes or until thoroughly heated.

46

Three-Pepper Quesadillas

SPINACH RICOTTA SPREAD

  1 qt. chopped fresh spinach
  ½ cup chopped onion
  1 (8 oz.) pkg. Light PHILADELPHIA
     BRAND Neufchatel Cheese,
     softened
  ¾ cup lowfat ricotta cheese
  ½ teaspoon dried basil leaves, crushed
  ½ teaspoon dried oregano leaves,
     crushed
  ¼ teaspoon salt
  ⅛ teaspoon garlic power
  ⅛ teaspoon pepper
  ¾ cup chopped tomato
  2 tablespoons KRAFT 100% Grated
     Parmesan Cheese

- Preheat oven to 350°.
- Place spinach and onions in small saucepan. Cover; cook 5 minutes or until tender.
- Beat cheeses and seasonings in small mixing bowl at medium speed with electric mixer until well blended. Stir in spinach mixture; spread into 9-inch pie plate.
- Bake 15 to 20 minutes or until thoroughly heated. Top with remaining ingredients. Serve with crisp rye crackers or bagel chips. *12 servings*

Prep time: 15 minutes
Cooking time: 20 minutes

MICROWAVE: • Place spinach and onions in 2-quart casserole; cover. Microwave on HIGH 3 to 4 minutes or until tender; drain.
• Beat cheeses and seasonings in small mixing bowl at medium speed with electric mixer until well blended. Stir in spinach mixture; spread into 9-inch pie plate.
• Microwave on HIGH 4 to 6 minutes or until thoroughly heated, stirring every 2 minutes. Stir before serving. Top with remaining ingredients. Serve with crisp rye crackers or bagel chips.

Microwave cooking time: 10 minutes

INDONESIAN SATAY

  4 (approx. 2 lbs.) boneless, skinless
     chicken breasts, cut into strips
  ¼ cup lime juice
  2 garlic cloves, minced
  1 teaspoon grated lime peel
  ½ teaspoon ground ginger
  ½ teaspoon cayenne pepper
     Spicy Peanut Sauce

- Marinate chicken in lime juice, garlic, peel, ginger and pepper in refrigerator 1 hour.
- Prepare coals for grilling.
- Thread chicken on individual wooden skewers; place on greased grill over hot coals (coals will be glowing). Grill, uncovered, 3 to 5 minutes on each side or until tender. Serve with Spicy Peanut Sauce. *15 servings*

SPICY PEANUT SAUCE
  1 (8 oz.) pkg. PHILADELPHIA
     BRAND Cream Cheese, cubed
  ½ cup milk
  3 tablespoons peanut butter
  2 tablespoons packed brown sugar
  ½ teaspoon ground cardamom
  ⅛ teaspoon cayenne pepper

- Stir together ingredients in small saucepan over low heat until smooth.

Prep time: 20 minutes plus marinating
Cooking time: 10 minutes

Variation: Prepare chicken as directed except for grilling. Place skewers on rack of broiler pan. Broil 10 to 15 minutes or until tender, turning halfway through cooking time.

48

Indonesian Satay

APRICOT FRAPPÉ

For a chilled, frosty effect, serve in glasses that have been placed in the freezer for about 10 minutes

> 2 cups apricot nectar
> ½ cup Light PHILADELPHIA BRAND Pasteurized Process Cream Cheese Product
> 1 cup diet ginger ale
> 3 tablespoons orange juice or orange-flavored liqueur
> ½ teaspoon vanilla
> 3 ice cubes

- Gradually add nectar to cream cheese product in food processor or blender container; process until blended.
- Add ginger ale, orange juice and vanilla; process until well blended. Add ice; process 1 minute. Garnish with fresh fruit, if desired.   *6 servings*

Prep time: 10 minutes

STRAWBERRY FROSTY

A delightful way to enjoy fresh strawberries.

> 1 (8 oz.) container PHILADELPHIA BRAND Soft Cream Cheese with Strawberries
> 1 pt. strawberries, hulled
> 1 cup frozen strawberry lowfat yogurt
> 1 cup diet lemon-lime carbonated beverage
> 1 tablespoon sugar or 3 packets sugar substitute

- Place cream cheese and strawberries in food processor or blender container; process until blended.
- Add frozen yogurt, carbonated beverage and sugar; process until well blended. Serve over ice, if desired.   *6 servings*

Prep time: 15 minutes

HERB & GARLIC BITES

Finely chopped ham or crumbled, crisply cooked bacon, are delicious alternatives to pepperoni.

> 2 (7.5 oz.) cans refrigerated buttermilk biscuits
> 1 (8 oz.) container PHILADELPHIA BRAND Soft Cream Cheese with Herb & Garlic
> 6 ozs. pepperoni, finely chopped
> 1 egg, beaten

- Preheat oven to 400°.
- Separate each biscuit in half. Gently stretch dough to form 3-inch circles.
- Stir together cream cheese and pepperoni in small bowl until well blended. Spoon 1½ teaspoons cream cheese mixture onto center of each circle. Fold in half; press edges together to seal.
- Place on cookie sheet. Brush with egg. Bake 8 to 10 minutes or until golden brown. Serve immediately.
  Approximately 3½ dozen

Prep time: 10 minutes
Cooking time: 10 minutes

51

SPA TORTILLAS

The combination of crunchy, fresh vegetables, PHILLY Cream Cheese and spicy seasonings is the filling for these tasty tortillas.

> 1 (8 oz.) container Light
>   PHILADELPHIA BRAND
>   Pasteurized Process Cream Cheese
>   Product
> 2 teaspoons chili power
> 1 teaspoon dried oregano leaves,
>   crushed
> ½ teaspoon ground cumin
> ¼ teaspoon hot pepper sauce
> 1 cup coarsely chopped tomato
> ½ cup coarsely chopped cucumber
> ½ cup small broccoli flowerets
> ½ cup coarsely chopped carrots
> ¼ cup green onion slices
> 2 tablespoon chopped green pepper
> 8 (6-inch) flour tortillas

- Preheat oven 325°.
- Stir together cream cheese product and seasonings in large bowl until well blended. Add vegetables; mix well.
- Wrap tortillas in foil. Bake 15 minutes.
- Spoon ⅓ cup vegetable mixture onto each tortilla; roll up. Serve with salsa, if desired.   *4 servings*

Prep time: 15 minutes
Cooking time: 15 minutes

CHEESE & NUT LOG

Pistachios add flair to this great make-ahead recipe.

> 1½ cups (6 ozs.) KRAFT Shredded
>   Sharp Cheddar Cheese
> 4 ozs. PHILADELPHIA BRAND Cream
>   Cheese, softened
> 2 tablespoons finely chopped green
>   onion
> 2 tablespoons finely chopped red
>   pepper
> 1 small garlic clove, minced
> 2 teaspoons white wine worcestershire
>   sauce
> 4 ozs. PHILADELPHIA BRAND Cream
>   Cheese, softened
> ½ cup (2 ozs.) KRAFT Blue Cheese
>   Crumbles
> 2 tablespoons milk
> ⅓ cup finely chopped red or natural
>   pistachio nuts

- Beat cheddar cheese and 4 ounces cream cheese in small mixing bowl at medium speed with electric mixer until well blended. Add onions, peppers, garlic and worcestershire sauce; mix well. Chill 30 minutes.
- Beat remaining 4 ounces cream cheese, blue cheese and milk in small mixing bowl at medium speed with electric mixer until well blended.
- Shape cheddar cheese mixture into 8-inch log. Spread blue cheese mixture evenly over top and sides of log. Cover with pistachio nuts. Chill several hours.
                    10 to 12 servings

Prep time: 20 minutes plus chilling

52

Cheese & Nut Log

HAM & DIJON PASTRY CUPS

1 (17¼ oz.) pkg. frozen ready-to-bake
    puff pastry sheets, thawed
1 (8 oz.) container PHILADELPHIA
    BRAND Soft Cream Cheese with
    Chives and Onion
1 cup (4 ozs.) KRAFT Shredded Swiss
    Cheese
4 OSCAR MAYER Smoked Cooked
    Ham Slices, chopped
⅓ cup chopped red pepper
1 egg, beaten
2 tablespoons Dijon mustard

- Preheat oven to 425°.
- On lightly floured surface, roll puff pastry
  into two 12×9-inch rectangles. Cut each
  rectangle into twelve 3-inch squares.
- Place pastry squares, with pastry corners
  pointing up, in cups of medium-size
  muffin pan.
- Stir together remaining ingredients in
  medium bowl until well blended. Spoon
  1 tablespoonful cheese mixture into each
  pastry cup.
- Bake 15 to 18 minutes or until pastry is
  golden brown.   *2 dozen*

Prep time: 20 minutes
Cooking time: 18 minutes

CRISPY WONTONS WITH ORIENTAL DIPPING SAUCE

*Sesame oil and Chinese rice wine add a
unique blend of flavors to this recipe. To
make ahead, wrap assembled wontons
securely in plastic wrap and refrigerate
until ready to bake.*

½ lb. ground pork, cooked, well drained
1 (8 oz.) container PHILADELPHIA
    BRAND Soft Cream Cheese with
    Chives & Onion
1 teaspoon chopped peeled fresh
    ginger root
1 teaspoon sesame oil
32 wonton wrappers
    Sesame seeds
    Oriental Dipping Sauce

- Preheat oven to 425°.
- Mix together meat, cream cheese, ginger
  and sesame oil in medium bowl until well
  blended.
- Place 1 tablespoon meat mixture in center
  of each wonton wrapper. Bring corners
  together over meat mixture; twist. Pinch
  together to enclose meat in wonton
  wrapper. Flatten bottom. Repeat with
  remaining meat mixture and wonton
  wrappers.
- Place in 15×10×1-inch jelly roll pan.
  Brush lightly with water; sprinkle with
  sesame seeds.
- Bake 10 to 12 minutes or until golden
  brown. Remove from pan; drain on paper
  towels. Serve with Oriental Dipping
  Sauce.   *32 appetizers*

ORIENTAL DIPPING SAUCE

2 tablespoons soy sauce
1 tablespoon Chinese rice wine
1 tablespoon cold water

- Stir together ingredients in small bowl
  until well blended.

Prep time: 25 minutes
Cooking time: 12 minutes

54

Crispy Wontons with Oriental Dipping Sauce

BREAD STICKS BELLISIMA

A great snack ... simple and unique!

> **OSCAR MAYER Boiled Ham Slices**
> **PHILADELPHIA BRAND Soft Cream**
>   **Cheese with Herb & Garlic**
> **Bread sticks**

- Spread each ham slice with cream cheese; cut lengthwise into ½-inch strips. Wrap ham around bread sticks.

GONE BANANAS SHAKE

Garnish shakes with chocolate-dipped banana slices.

> **1½ cups skim milk**
> **½ cup Light PHILADELPHIA BRAND**
>   **Pasteurized Process Cream Cheese**
>   **Product**
> **1 large banana, cut into chunks**
> **3 tablespoons chocolate syrup**
> **6 ice cubes**

- Gradually add milk to cream cheese product in food processor or blender container; process until blended.
- Add bananas and syrup; process until well blended. Add ice; process 1 minute.

4 servings

Prep time: 10 minutes

ZESTY CORNCAKES

A savory variation of corn fritters, these versatile corncakes are delicious when served as appetizers, snacks or main-dish accompaniments.

> **2 (8 oz.) pkgs. PHILADELPHIA**
>   **BRAND Cream Cheese, softened**
> **¼ cup green onion slices**
>   **Salsa**
> **1 egg**
> **1 (10 oz.) pkg. BIRDS EYE Sweet**
>   **Corn, thawed, drained**
> **⅔ cup (3 ozs.) KRAFT Shredded Sharp**
>   **Cheddar Cheese**
>   **Cornmeal**
> **¼ cup flour**
> **1 teaspoon CALUMET Baking Powder**
> **1 teaspoon salt**
> **2 tablespoons PARKAY Margarine**
> **2 tablespoons oil**

- Beat cream cheese and onions in large mixing bowl at medium speed with electric mixer until well blended.
- Divide mixture in half; reserve one half for topping. Add ⅓ cup salsa and egg to remaining half, mixing until well blended.
- Stir in corn, cheddar cheese, ⅓ cup cornmeal, flour, baking powder and salt.
- Roll heaping tablespoonfuls of corn mixture in additional cornmeal; flatten dough into patties.
- Heat margarine and oil in large skillet. Add patties; cook until browned on both sides.
- Serve warm with reserved cream cheese mixture and additional salsa.

Approximately 2 dozen

Prep time: 30 minutes
Cooking time: 15 minutes

◆◆◆

For easy handling, roll formed balls in cornmeal; flatten in skillet with back of spatula.

Zesty Corncakes

GREEK ISLES APPETIZERS

For extra convenience, prepare the meatballs ahead of time and freeze.

  1 lb. ground beef
  1 lb. ground lamb
  2 eggs
  ½ cup finely chopped onion
  2 garlic cloves, minced
  2 teaspoons dry mustard
  1 teaspoon dried thyme leaves, crushed
  1 teaspoon ground coriander
  ½ teaspoon salt
  ½ teaspoon pepper
    Cucumber Sauce

- Preheat oven to 350°.
- Mix together meat, eggs, onions, garlic and seasonings in large bowl until well blended. Shape into 1-inch balls. Place on rack in 15×10×1-inch jelly roll pan.
- Bake 15 to 20 minutes or until lightly browned. Serve with Cucumber Sauce.

Approximately 6 dozen

CUCUMBER SAUCE

  1 (8 oz.) container PHILADELPHIA BRAND Soft Cream Cheese with Herb & Garlic
  ½ cup plain yogurt
  1 tablespoon lemon juice
  ½ cup shredded cucumber, well drained

- Stir together cream cheese, yogurt and lemon juice in small bowl until well blended. Stir in cucumber.

Prep time: 35 minutes plus chilling
Cooking time: 20 minutes

MICROWAVE: • Mix together meat, eggs, onions, garlic and seasonings in large bowl until well blended. Shape into 1-inch balls. Place half of meatballs in 9-inch pie plate; cover with waxed paper. • Microwave on HIGH 4 to 8 minutes or until centers are no longer pink, rearranging every 3 minutes. Drain. • Repeat with remaining meatballs. Serve with Cucumber Sauce.

Microwave cooking time: 16 minutes

58

MEDITERRANEAN APPETIZER

  1 (8 oz.) container Light PHILADELPHIA BRAND Pasteurized Process Cream Cheese Product
  2 teaspoons red wine vinegar
  1 garlic clove, minced
  ½ teaspoon dried oregano leaves, crushed
  ½ teaspoon lemon pepper seasoning
 24 (3-inch) lahvosh crackers or 4 pita bread rounds, split
  1½ cups finely torn spinach
  1 tomato, chopped
  4 ozs. CHURNY ATHENOS Feta Cheese, crumbled
  ½ cup Greek ripe olives, pitted, chopped

- Stir together cream cheese product, vinegar, garlic and seasonings in small bowl until well blended.
- Spread crackers with cream cheese mixture. Top with remaining ingredients.

8 servings

Prep time: 20 minutes

Variation: Substitute one 15-inch lahvosh cracker bread for individual crackers. Prepare according to package directions.

Lahvosh is a Middle Eastern sesame seed crisp cracker bread. Traditionally eaten as a cracker, it can be softened by holding under cold water, then placing between two damp towels for about 1 hour.

Mediterranean Appetizer

SALAMI & CHEESE TOPPED PITA CHIPS

1 (8 oz.) container PHILADELPHIA BRAND Soft Cream Cheese
1 cup (4 ozs.) KRAFT Shredded Low-Moisture Part-Skim Mozzarella Cheese
½ cup chopped OSCAR MAYER Hard Salami Slices
1 small tomato, seeded, chopped
⅛ teaspoon pepper
  Toasted pita wedges

- Stir together cheeses, salami, tomatoes and pepper in medium bowl until well blended.
- Top each pita wedge with 1 rounded teaspoonful cheese mixture. Place on cookie sheet.
- Broil 3 to 4 minutes or until cheese is melted. *Approximately 4 dozen*

Prep time: 10 minutes
Cooking time: 4 minutes

CRANBERRY COOL

2 cups low-calorie cranberry apple drink
½ cup Light PHILADELPHIA BRAND Pasteurized Process Cream Cheese Product
1 cup frozen vanilla lowfat yogurt

- Gradually add cranberry apple drink to cream cheese product in food processor or blender container; process until blended.
- Add frozen yogurt; process until well blended. Serve over ice, if desired.
  4 servings

Prep time: 10 minutes

PIZZA ROLL

1 (1 lb.) loaf frozen Italian bread dough, thawed
1 (8 oz.) container PHILADELPHIA BRAND Soft Cream Cheese with Herb & Garlic
1½ cups (6 ozs.) KRAFT Shredded Low-Moisture Part-Skim Mozzarella Cheese
¾ cup (3 ozs.) chopped pepperoni
⅓ cup finely chopped green pepper
1 tablespoon olive oil
½ teaspoon Italian seasoning

- Roll dough to 15×10-inch rectangle on floured surface. Spread cream cheese over dough to within 1 inch of edges.
- Sprinkle mozzarella cheese, pepperoni and peppers over cream cheese. Roll up dough from long side; press edges together to seal. Brush top and sides with olive oil; sprinkle with seasoning.
- Cover; let rise in warm place 1 hour.
- Preheat oven to 350°.
- Bake 30 to 35 minutes or until golden brown. *10 to 12 servings*

Prep time: 25 minutes plus rising
Cooking time: 35 minutes

60

Pizza Roll

INDIVIDUAL HERB–CHEESE TORTES

1 (4 oz.) cup PHILADELPHIA BRAND Whipped Cream Cheese with Chives
3 tablespoons KRAFT 100% Grated Parmesan Cheese
1 tablespoon finely chopped fresh basil or ½ teaspoon dried basil leaves, crushed
1 (4 oz.) cup PHILADELPHIA BRAND Whipped Cream Cheese
2 OSCAR MAYER Smoked Cooked Ham Slices, finely chopped
½ teaspoon coarsely ground black pepper
60 table wafer crackers
2 tablespoons finely chopped fresh parsley
1 hard-cooked egg yolk, sieved

- Stir together cream cheese with chives, parmesan cheese and basil in small bowl until well blended.
- Stir together plain cream cheese, ham and pepper in small bowl until well blended.
- Spread 1 teaspoonful parmesan cheese mixture onto one cracker; spread 1 teaspoonful ham mixture onto second cracker. Stack crackers. Repeat with remaining spreads and crackers.
- Toss together parsley and yolk in small bowl; sprinkle over appetizers. Garnish with fresh herbs, if desired.   *2½ dozen*

Prep time: 25 minutes

CHUTNEY CUCUMBER ROUNDS

1 (8 oz.) pkg. PHILADELPHIA BRAND Cream Cheese, cubed
2 tablespoons mango chutney
1 tablespoon chopped peeled fresh ginger root
1 garlic clove
2 to 3 European or English cucumbers
¼ cup green onion slices

- Place cream cheese, chutney, ginger and garlic in food processor or blender container; process until well blended. Chill.
- Diagonally slice cucumbers ½ inch thick. Scoop indentation in center of each slice with melon baller or teaspoon.
- Fill with cream cheese mixture. Sprinkle with onions. Chill.
                    Approximately 3 dozen

Prep time: 20 minutes plus chilling

HOT AND SPICY CHICKEN NUGGETS

This creamy salsa dip is a natural accompaniment for popular chicken nuggets.

1 (8 oz.) container PHILADELPHIA BRAND Soft Cream Cheese
½ cup salsa
2 tablespoons milk
½ teaspoon ground cumin
½ teaspoon onion powder
½ teaspoon garlic powder
¼ to ½ teaspoon cayenne pepper
2 (10.5 oz.) pkgs. frozen chicken nuggets

- Stir together all ingredients except chicken nuggets in small bowl until well blended. Chill.
- Prepare chicken nuggets according to package directions. Serve with cream cheese dip.   *Approximately 3 dozen*

Prep time: 10 minutes plus chilling
Cooking time: Approximately 20 minutes

62

Individual Herb-Cheese Tortes

From Breakfast-to-Dessert Breads

BREAKFAST RAISIN RING

PHILLY Cream Cheese adds a delicate flavor and texture to this coffeecake and filling.

 1 (8 oz.) pkg. PHILADELPHIA
   BRAND Cream Cheese, cubed
 1 cup cold water
 1 (16 oz.) pkg. hot roll mix
 1 egg
 1 teaspoon vanilla
 ½ cup packed brown sugar
 ⅓ cup PARKAY Margarine
 ¼ cup granulated sugar
 1½ teaspoons ground cinnamon
 1½ teaspoons vanilla
 ½ cup golden raisins
   Vanilla Drizzle

- Preheat oven to 350°.
- Blend 6 ounces cream cheese and water in small saucepan. Cook over low heat until mixture reaches 115° to 120°, stirring occasionally.
- Stir together hot roll mix and yeast packet in large bowl. Add cream cheese mixture, egg and 1 teaspoon vanilla, mixing until dough pulls away from sides of bowl.
- Knead dough on lightly floured surface 5 minutes or until smooth and elastic. Cover; let rise in warm place 20 minutes.
- Beat remaining cream cheese, brown sugar, margarine, granulated sugar, cinnamon and 1½ teaspoons vanilla in small mixing bowl at medium speed with electric mixer until well blended.
- Roll out dough to 20×12-inch rectangle; spread cream cheese mixture over dough to within 1½ inches from outer edges of dough. Sprinkle with raisins.
- Roll up from long end, sealing edges. Place, seam side down, on greased cookie sheet; shape into ring, pressing ends together to seal. Make 1-inch cuts through ring from outer edge at 2-inch intervals. Cover; let rise in warm place 30 minutes.
- Bake 30 to 40 minutes or until golden brown. Cool slightly. Drizzle with Vanilla Drizzle.   *8 to 10 servings*

VANILLA DRIZZLE

 1 cup powdered sugar
 1 to 2 tablespoons milk
 1 teaspoon vanilla
 ½ teaspoon ground cinnamon
   (optional)

- Stir ingredients together in small bowl until smooth.

Prep time: 30 minutes plus rising
Cooking time: 40 minutes

To knead dough, place on lightly floured surface. With floured hands, fold dough toward you with fingers; push firmly away with heel of hand. Give dough a quarter turn; repeat. Add additional flour to surface as needed to prevent sticking.

Breakfast Raisin Ring

HOME–STYLE BLUEBERRY MUFFINS

PHILLY Cream Cheese makes these much more than "just muffins."

- 1 (8 oz.) pkg. PHILADELPHIA BRAND Cream Cheese, softened
- ¼ cup sugar
- 1 egg yolk
- 1 teaspoon vanilla
- 1 (23.5 oz.) pkg. bakery-style blueberry muffin mix
- ¾ cup cold water
- 1 egg
- 1 teaspoon grated lemon peel
- 1 teaspoon ground cinnamon

- Preheat oven to 400°.
- Beat cream cheese, sugar, egg yolk and vanilla in small mixing bowl at medium speed with electric mixer until well blended.
- Rinse and drain blueberries from muffin mix. Stir together muffin mix, water, egg and peel in large bowl (mixture will be lumpy). Stir in blueberries. Pour into well-greased medium-size muffin pan.
- Spoon cream cheese mixture over batter; sprinkle with combined topping mix and cinnamon.
- Bake 18 to 22 minutes or until lightly browned. Cool 5 minutes. Loosen muffins from rim of pan; cool before removing from pan.   *1 dozen*

Prep time: 20 minutes
Cooking time: 22 minutes

Tough muffins full of holes are the result of overmixing. For tender muffins, make a well in the combined dry ingredients. Pour combined liquids, all at once, into the well. Stir just enough to moisten dry ingredients. Do not overmix.

CARAMEL–PECAN STICKY BUNS

PHILLY Cream Cheese adds its special flavor to the dough.

- 1 (8 oz.) pkg. PHILADELPHIA BRAND Cream Cheese, cubed
- ¾ cup cold water
- 1 (16 oz.) pkg. hot roll mix
- 1 egg
- ⅓ cup granulated sugar
- 1 teaspoon ground cinnamon
- 1 cup pecan halves
- ¾ cup packed brown sugar
- ½ cup light corn syrup
- ¼ cup PARKAY Margarine, melted

- Preheat oven to 350°.
- Stir together 6 ounces cream cheese and water in small saucepan. Cook over low heat until mixture reaches 115° to 120°, stirring occasionally.
- Stir together hot roll mix and yeast packet in large bowl. Add cream cheese mixture and egg, mixing until dough pulls away from sides of bowl.
- Knead dough on lightly floured surface 5 minutes or until smooth and elastic. Cover; let rise in warm place 20 minutes.
- Beat remaining cream cheese, granulated sugar and cinnamon in small mixing bowl at medium speed with electric mixer until well blended.
- Roll out dough to 18×12-inch rectangle; spread cream cheese mixture over dough to within 1 inch from outer edges of dough.
- Roll up from long end, sealing edges. Cut into twenty-four ¾-inch slices.
- Stir together remaining ingredients in small bowl. Spoon 2 teaspoonfuls pecan mixture into bottoms of greased medium-sized muffin pans.
- Place dough, cut side up, in cups. Cover; let rise in warm place 30 minutes.
- Bake 20 to 25 minutes or until golden brown. Invert onto serving platter immediately.   *2 dozen*

Prep time: 30 minutes plus rising
Cooking time: 25 minutes

66

67

Top to bottom: Home-Style Blueberry Muffins;
Caramel-Pecan Sticky Buns

HERB & TWO–CHEESE BREAD

1 (8 oz.) pkg. PHILADELPHIA
    BRAND Cream Cheese, softened
2 tablespoons PARKAY Margarine
1 tablespoon sugar
2 eggs
½ cup milk
1½ cups (6 ozs.) KRAFT Shredded
    Sharp Cheddar Cheese
1 tablespoon green onion slices
2 cups flour
2 teaspoons CALUMET Baking Powder
¾ teaspoon Italian seasoning
¼ teaspoon salt

- Preheat oven to 350°.
- Beat cream cheese, margarine and sugar in large mixing bowl at medium speed with electric mixer until well blended. Add eggs and milk; mix well.
- Toss together cheese and onions with combined dry ingredients in large bowl. Add cream cheese mixture, mixing just until moistened. (Mixture will be thick.)
- Pour into greased and floured 9×5-inch loaf pan.
- Bake 45 to 50 minutes or until golden brown. Cool 5 minutes; remove from pan. Cool completely.　　　　*1 loaf*

Prep time: 20 minutes
Cooking time: 50 minutes

CREAM CHEESE AND PECAN DANISH

1 sheet frozen ready-to-bake puff
    pastry, thawed
2 (3 oz.) pkgs. PHILADELPHIA
    BRAND Cream Cheese, softened
¼ cup powdered sugar
1 egg
1 teaspoon vanilla
¾ cup chopped pecans
    Creamy Glaze

- Preheat oven to 375°.
- Unfold pastry; roll to 15×10-inch rectangle. Place in 15×10×1-inch jelly roll pan.
- Beat 6 ounces cream cheese, ¼ cup sugar, egg and vanilla in small mixing bowl at medium speed with electric mixer until well blended. Stir in ½ cup pecans.
- Spread cream cheese mixture over pastry to within 3 inches from outer edges.
- Make 2-inch cuts at 1-inch intervals on long sides of pastry. Crisscross strips over filling.
- Bake 25 to 30 minutes or until golden brown. Cool.
- Drizzle with Creamy Glaze. Sprinkle with remaining pecans.　　*10 to 12 servings*

CREAMY GLAZE

1 (3 oz.) pkg. PHILADELPHIA
    BRAND Cream Cheese, softened
¾ cup powdered sugar
1 tablespoon milk

- Beat ingredients until smooth.

Prep time: 20 minutes
Cooking time: 30 minutes

68

Cream Cheese and Pecan Danish

ORANGE RUM BABA

1 (8 oz.) pkg. PHILADELPHIA
   BRAND Cream Cheese, cubed
1 cup orange juice
2 tablespoons PARKAY Margarine
2 tablespoons sugar
1 teaspoon grated orange peel
1 tablespoon rum
1 (16 oz.) pkg. hot roll mix
1 egg
2 cups cold water
1 cup sugar
3 tablespoons rum
2 tablespoons vanilla
   Orange Glaze

- Preheat oven to 350°.
- Stir together cream cheese, juice, margarine, 2 tablespoons sugar and peel in small saucepan. Cook over low heat until mixture reaches 115° to 120°, stirring occasionally. Stir in 1 tablespoon rum.
- Stir together hot roll mix and yeast packet in large bowl. Add cream cheese mixture and egg, mixing until dough pulls away from sides of bowl.
- Knead dough on lightly floured surface 5 minutes or until smooth and elastic. Cover; let rise in warm place 20 minutes.
- Place dough in greased 6½-cup ring mold. Cover; let rise in warm place until doubled in volume, about 35 minutes.
- Bake 30 to 35 minutes or until golden brown. Cool slightly.
- Stir together water and 1 cup sugar in small saucepan over low heat until sugar is dissolved. Stir in 3 tablespoons rum and vanilla. Reserve ¾ cup syrup for use in Orange Glaze.
- Prick cake several times with fork. Pour 1 cup remaining syrup over cake; let stand 15 minutes. Invert onto rimmed plate; prick cake several times with fork. Pour remaining syrup over cake. Drizzle with Orange Glaze. Serve with whipped cream and seasonal fruit, if desired.

10 to 12 servings

ORANGE GLAZE

¾ cup reserved syrup
1 tablespoon cornstarch
1 teaspoon orange zest

- Gradually add reserved syrup to cornstarch in small saucepan.
- Bring to boil over medium heat, stirring constantly. Boil 1 minute. Stir in zest.

Prep time: 45 minutes plus rising
Cooking time: 35 minutes

◆ ◆ ◆

Ovens are ideal for rising yeast breads. A gas oven warmed by the pilot light or an electric oven turned to the lowest setting 1 minute, then turned off, will provide enough warmth for rising.

Orange Rum Baba

FRUIT & CITRUS SCONES

A tradition at English tea, these scones taste best when served warm, spread with PHILADELPHIA BRAND Soft Cream Cheese with Pineapple.

  2 cups flour
⅓ cup packed brown sugar
2½ teaspoons CALUMET Baking Powder
  ¼ teaspoon salt
  ½ cup PARKAY Margarine
  ¾ cup diced mixed dried fruit
  2 tablespoons grated orange peel
  4 ozs. PHILADELPHIA BRAND Cream Cheese, softened
  Milk

- Preheat oven to 400°.
- Stir together dry ingredients in medium bowl; cut in margarine until mixture resembles coarse crumbs. Stir in dried fruit and peel.
- Mix cream cheese and ¼ cup milk in small bowl until well blended. Add to dry ingredients, mixing just until moistened. Add additional milk, 1 tablespoon at a time, mixing until dough forms ball. Knead ten times.
- On floured surface, roll dough to 12×9-inch rectangle. Cut into twelve 3-inch squares; cut each square diagonally in half. Place on greased cookie sheet.
- Bake 12 to 15 minutes or until lightly browned. Serve warm.　　*2 dozen*

Prep time: 15 minutes
Cooking time: 15 minutes

EASTER BUNS WITH VANILLA GLAZE

A special Easter treat… PHILLY Soft Cream Cheese with Pineapple and piña colada yogurt add the unique rich flavor and texture to these delicious rolls.

  1 (8 oz.) container PHILADELPHIA BRAND Soft Cream Cheese with Pineapple
  1 (8 oz.) container piña colada-flavored yogurt
  2 tablespoons PARKAY Margarine
  1 (16 oz.) pkg. hot roll mix
⅓ cup granulated sugar
  1 egg
  Vanilla Glaze

- Preheat oven to 350°.
- Stir together cream cheese, yogurt and margarine in small saucepan until well blended. Cook over low heat until mixture reaches 115° to 120°, stirring occasionally.
- Stir together hot roll mix, yeast packet and granulated sugar in large bowl. Add cream cheese mixture and egg, mixing until dough pulls away from sides of bowl.
- Knead dough on lightly floured surface 5 minutes or until smooth and elastic. Cover; let rise in warm place 20 minutes.
- Divide dough into twenty four balls. Place 2 inches apart on greased cookie sheets. Cut crisscross design with knife on top of balls, ½ inch deep. Cover; let rise in warm place 30 minutes.
- Bake 20 to 22 minutes or until lightly browned. Dip warm buns into Vanilla Glaze.　　*2 dozen*

VANILLA GLAZE

1½ cups powdered sugar
  3 tablespoons light corn syrup
  3 tablespoons cold water
  2 teaspoons vanilla

- Stir together ingredients in small bowl until smooth.

Prep time: 30 minutes plus rising
Cooking time: 22 minutes

72

Easter Buns with Vanilla Glase

LEMON CRANBERRY LOAF

1 (8 oz.) pkg. PHILADELPHIA
   BRAND Cream Cheese, softened
⅓ cup PARKAY Margarine
1¼ cups sugar
1 teaspoon vanilla
3 eggs
2 tablespoons lemon juice
1 teaspoon grated lemon peel
1½ cups chopped cranberries
2¼ cups flour
2 teaspoons CALUMET Baking Powder
½ teaspoon baking soda

- Preheat oven to 325°.
- Beat cream cheese, margarine, sugar and vanilla in large mixing bowl at medium speed with electric mixer until well blended. Add eggs, one at a time, mixing well after each addition. Stir in lemon juice and peel.
- Toss together cranberries with combined dry ingredients in large bowl. Add cream cheese mixture, mixing just until moistened.
- Pour into greased and floured 9×5-inch loaf pan. Bake 1 hour and 15 minutes. Cool 5 minutes; remove from pan. Cool completely.   *1 loaf*

Prep time: 15 minutes
Cooking time: 1 hour and 15 minutes

PEAR CREAM BREAKFAST CAKE

Incredibly delicious ... perfect for brunch or as a delicious dessert.

1 (29 oz.) can pear halves in heavy
   syrup, undrained
1 (8 oz.) pkg. PHILADELPHIA
   BRAND Cream Cheese, softened
¼ cup KRAFT Apricot Preserves
2 tablespoons PARKAY Margarine
1 (9 oz.) pkg. yellow cake mix
2 tablespoons oil
1 egg
1 teaspoon ground ginger

- Preheat oven to 350°.
- Drain pears, reserving ½ cup syrup. Slice pears; place on bottom of 8-inch square baking pan.
- Beat cream cheese, preserves and margarine in small mixing bowl at medium speed with electric mixer until well blended; pour over pears.
- Beat cake mix, reserved syrup, oil, egg and ginger in large mixing bowl at medium speed with electric mixer until well blended; pour over cream cheese mixture.
- Bake 35 to 40 minutes or until golden brown. Serve warm with half and half.
                    8 to 10 servings

Prep time: 15 minutes
Cooking time: 40 minutes

74

Pear Cream Breakfast Cake

CARDAMOM BRAID

1 (8 oz.) pkg. PHILADELPHIA
  BRAND Cream Cheese, cubed
⅔ cup cold water
1 (16 oz.) pkg. hot roll mix
⅓ cup sugar
1 teaspoon ground cardamom
1 egg, beaten
1 to 2 tablespoons milk
1 tablespoon sugar

- Place cream cheese and water in small saucepan. Cook over low heat until mixture reaches 115° to 120°, stirring occasionally until smooth. Remove from heat.
- Stir together hot roll mix, yeast packet, ⅓ cup sugar and cardamom in large bowl. Add cream cheese mixture and egg, mixing until dough pulls away from sides of bowl.
- On floured surface, knead dough 5 minutes or until smooth and elastic. Cover; let rest in warm place 20 minutes.
- Divide dough into thirds. Roll each third into 16-inch rope; braid, pinching ends together to seal. Place braid on greased cookie sheet.
- Cover; let rise in warm place 30 minutes. Brush with milk; sprinkle with 1 tablespoon sugar.
- Preheat oven to 375°.
- Bake 25 to 30 minutes or until light golden brown. Serve with PHILADELPHIA BRAND Soft Cream Cheese and KRAFT Apricot Preserves, if desired.   *1 loaf*

Prep time: 20 minutes plus rising
Cooking time: 30 minutes

Variation: Add one (6 oz.) package diced mixed dried fruit to dry ingredients.

◆ ◆ ◆

Cardamom, a member of the ginger family, is an aromatic, sweet spice. Popular in India and Scandinavian countries, it is used in much the same way we use cinnamon-sugar blends.

CINNAMON-SWIRL BREAD

1 (8 oz.) pkg. PHILADELPHIA
  BRAND Cream Cheese, softened
⅔ cup cold water
1 teaspoon vanilla
1 (16 oz.) pkg. hot roll mix
⅓ cup sugar
1 egg, beaten
1 tablespoon PARKAY Margarine,
  melted
½ cup sugar
2 teaspoons ground cinnamon
  Vanilla Icing

- Place cream cheese and water in small saucepan. Cook over low heat until mixture reaches 115° to 120°, stirring occasionally until smooth. Remove from heat. Stir in vanilla.
- Stir together hot roll mix, yeast packet and ⅓ cup sugar in large bowl. Add cream cheese mixture and egg, mixing until dough pulls away from sides of bowl.
- On floured surface, knead dough 5 minutes or until smooth and elastic. Cover; let rest in warm place 30 minutes.
- On floured surface, roll out dough to 15×7-inch rectangle. Brush with margarine; sprinkle with combined ½ cup sugar and cinnamon.
- Roll up dough from short end; press ends together to seal. Fold ends under loaf; place, seam side down, in greased 9×5-inch loaf pan. Cover; let rise in warm place 30 minutes.
- Preheat oven to 350°.
- Bake 45 to 55 minutes or until bread sounds hollow when tapped. Remove from pan; cool completely. Drizzle with Vanilla Icing.   *1 loaf*

VANILLA ICING

1 cup powdered sugar
2 tablespoons milk
¼ teaspoon vanilla

- Stir together ingredients in small bowl until smooth.

Prep time: 20 minutes plus rising
Cooking time: 55 minutes

76

Top to bottom: Cardamom Braid; Cinnamon-Swirl Bread

FRENCH CUSTARD MORNING SQUARES

2 (8 oz.) pkgs. PHILADELPHIA
 BRAND Cream Cheese, softened
½ cup granulated sugar
1 teaspoon vanilla
1 egg, separated
2 (8 oz.) cans refrigerated quick
 crescent dinner rolls
Sifted powdered sugar

- Preheat oven to 350°.
- Beat cream cheese, granulated sugar, vanilla and egg yolk in large mixing bowl at medium speed with electric mixer until well blended.
- Place half of dough in 13×9-inch baking pan; press perforations together to seal. Bake 10 minutes.
- Pour cream cheese mixture over crust. Place remaining dough on waxed paper; roll to 13×9-inch rectangle. Invert dough onto cream cheese mixture; remove waxed paper. Brush top with beaten egg white.
- Bake 20 to 25 minutes or until golden brown. Cool. Sprinkle with powdered sugar.   *12 to 15 servings*

Prep time: 20 minutes
Cooking time: 25 minutes

CHERRY CREAM CHEESE COFFEECAKE

Serve this delicious coffeecake warm with your favorite GENERAL FOODS International Coffee.

1½ cups flour
 1 cup old-fashioned or quick oats,
 uncooked
¾ cup sugar
¾ cup PARKAY Margarine
½ cup BREAKSTONE'S Sour Cream
 1 egg
½ teaspoon baking soda
 1 (8 oz.) pkg. PHILADELPHIA
 BRAND Cream Cheese, softened
¼ cup sugar
¼ teaspoon almond extract
 1 egg
¾ cup cherry pie filling
⅓ cup sliced almonds

- Preheat oven to 350°.
- Mix together flour, oats and ¾ cup sugar in large bowl; cut in margarine until mixture resembles coarse crumbs. Reserve 1 cup crumb mixture.
- Add sour cream, one egg and soda to remaining crumb mixture; mix well. Spread onto bottom and 2 inches up sides of greased 9-inch springform pan.
- Beat cream cheese, ¼ cup sugar and extract in small mixing bowl at medium speed with electric mixer until well blended. Blend in one egg. Pour into crust.
- Top with pie filling. Sprinkle with reserved crumb mixture and almonds.
- Bake 50 to 55 minutes or until golden brown. Cool 15 minutes. Carefully remove rim of pan. Serve warm or at room temperature.   *10 servings*

Prep time: 20 minutes
Cooking time: 55 minutes

Variation: Substitute KRAFT Red Raspberry Preserves for pie filling.

78

Cherry Cream Cheese Coffeecake

BANANA–SCOTCH BREAKFAST CAKE

1 (8 oz.) pkg. PHILADELPHIA
    BRAND Cream Cheese, softened
⅓ cup oil
2 eggs
½ teaspoon vanilla
½ cup cold water
1 (14 oz.) pkg. banana bread mix
½ cup chopped pecans, toasted
½ cup currants
1½ cups butterscotch morsels
    Powdered sugar

- Preheat oven to 350°.
- Beat cream cheese, oil, eggs and vanilla in large mixing bowl at medium speed with electric mixer until well blended. Gradually blend in water.
- Stir in bread mix, mixing just until moistened. Stir in pecans and currants. Pour into greased and floured 13×9-inch baking pan.
- Sprinkle with butterscotch morsels; gently press into batter.
- Bake 35 minutes or until wooden pick inserted in center comes out clean. Cool. Sprinkle lightly with powdered sugar just before serving.   *12 servings*

Prep time: 20 minutes
Cooking time: 35 minutes

80

PIÑA COLADA COFFEECAKE

¼ cup chopped almonds
¼ cup packed brown sugar
¼ cup BAKER'S ANGEL FLAKE
    Coconut
2 tablespoons flour
1 teaspoon ground cinnamon
1 (10 oz.) container frozen piña colada
    fruit mixer concentrate, thawed
1 (8 oz.) pkg. PHILADELPHIA
    BRAND Cream Cheese, softened
2 tablespoons lime juice
3 eggs
1 (18.25 oz.) pkg. white cake mix
    Lime Glaze

- Preheat oven to 350°.
- Stir together almonds, brown sugar, coconut, flour and cinnamon in small bowl.
- Reserve 3 tablespoons piña colada concentrate for use in Lime Glaze. Beat cream cheese, remaining concentrate and 2 tablespoons lime juice in large mixing bowl at medium speed with electric mixer until well blended.
- Add eggs, one at a time, mixing well after each addition. Add cake mix; beat until well blended.
- Pour half of batter into greased and floured 10-inch fluted tube pan. Sprinkle almond mixture over batter; top with remaining batter.
- Bake 55 to 60 minutes or until wooden pick inserted in center comes out clean. Cool. Drizzle with Lime Glaze.
          10 to 12 servings

LIME GLAZE

3 tablespoons reserved piña colada
    concentrate
2 teaspoons lime juice
1½ cups sifted powdered sugar

- Stir together reserved concentrate and 2 teaspoons lime juice in small bowl until smooth; gradually stir in powdered sugar.

Prep time: 25 minutes
Cooking time: 1 hour

SPICED PEAR AND PLUM KUCHEN

¼ cup PARKAY Margarine, melted
¼ cup packed brown sugar
½ teaspoon ground cinnamon
⅛ teaspoon ground cloves
2 pears, peeled, thinly sliced
1 (16 oz.) can whole purple plums in extra heavy syrup, drained, pitted
1 (8 oz.) pkg. PHILADELPHIA BRAND Cream Cheese, softened
½ cup PARKAY Margarine
1¼ cups granulated sugar
2 teaspoons vanilla
2 eggs
1¾ cups flour
1 teaspoon CALUMET Baking Powder
½ teaspoon baking soda
¼ teaspoon salt
¼ cup milk

* Preheat oven to 350°.
* Pour ¼ cup melted margarine into 9-inch square baking pan; brush sides and bottom of pan completely with margarine. Sprinkle combined brown sugar and spices over bottom of pan.
* Arrange pear slices, slightly overlapping, in circle on bottom of pan. Place plums in center and corners of pan.
* Beat cream cheese, ½ cup margarine, granulated sugar and vanilla in large mixing bowl at medium speed with electric mixer until well blended. Blend in eggs.
* Add combined dry ingredients alternately with milk, mixing well after each addition. Spread batter over fruit.
* Bake 1 hour or until wooden pick inserted in center comes out clean. Cool 10 minutes. Invert onto serving plate. Serve warm with half and half or milk.

12 servings

Prep time: 30 minutes
Cooking time: 1 hour

ORANGE DANISH COFFEECAKE

This easy coffeecake is a sure sensation for any gathering.

2 cups variety baking mix
¾ cup orange juice
½ cup granulated sugar
1 egg
1 (8 oz.) pkg. PHILADELPHIA BRAND Cream Cheese, softened
¼ cup granulated sugar
1 egg
1 teaspoon vanilla
⅓ cup packed brown sugar
⅓ cup chopped nuts
1 teaspoon grated orange peel
½ teaspoon ground cinnamon

* Preheat oven to 350°.
* Stir together baking mix, orange juice, ½ cup granulated sugar and one egg in medium bowl; pour into greased 9-inch square baking pan. Bake 10 minutes.
* Beat cream cheese, ¼ cup granulated sugar, one egg and vanilla in small mixing bowl at medium speed with electric mixer until well blended; pour over cake.
* Top with combined remaining ingredients.
* Bake 20 minutes.   *6 to 8 servings*

Prep time: 20 minutes
Cooking time: 20 minutes

Great Go-Alongs

SUMMER FRUIT MOLD

A tasty make-ahead salad for any gathering. Fill center of mold with your favorite fresh fruit.

> Cold water
> 2 (3 oz.) pkgs. JELL-O Brand Orange Flavor Sugar Free Gelatin
> 1 (20 oz.) can crushed pineapple in unsweetened juice, undrained
> 1 (8 oz.) container PHILADELPHIA BRAND Soft Cream Cheese
> 2 cups strawberry slices
> 1 (11 oz.) can mandarin orange segments, drained
> Leaf lettuce
> Assorted fresh fruit

- Bring 2 cups water to boil. Gradually add to gelatin in medium bowl; stir until dissolved.
- Drain pineapple, reserving juice. Add enough cold water to reserved juice to measure 1½ cups; stir into gelatin.
- Beat cream cheese in large mixing bowl at medium speed with electric mixer until smooth. Gradually add gelatin, mixing until well blended. Chill until thickened but not set; fold in fruit.
- Pour cream cheese mixture into lightly oiled 10- to 12-cup ring mold. Chill until firm.
- Unmold gelatin onto lettuce-covered platter; fill center with fresh fruit.
Approximately 12 servings

Prep time: 20 minutes plus chilling

RASPBERRY SPINACH SALAD

> 1 pt. raspberries
> 2 qts. torn spinach
> ½ cup chopped walnuts, toasted
> Raspberry Dressing

- Reserve ½ cup raspberries for Raspberry Dressing.
- Arrange spinach on individual plates; sprinkle with remaining raspberries and walnuts. Garnish as desired. Serve with dressing.
8 servings

RASPBERRY DRESSING

> 1 (8 oz.) pkg. Light PHILADELPHIA BRAND Neufchatel Cheese, softened
> ½ cup reserved raspberries
> ¼ cup raspberry vinegar or white wine vinegar
> 3 tablespoons sugar
> 1 tablespoon olive oil
> ¼ teaspoon salt

- Place ingredients in food processor or blender container; process until well blended.

Prep time: 15 minutes

To toast walnuts, preheat the oven to 350°. Bake walnuts in ungreased shallow pan 10 minutes or until lightly browned, stirring occasionally.

To toast walnuts in the microwave, place 1 tablespoon margarine in 9-inch pie plate. Microwave on HIGH 30 to 45 seconds or until margarine is melted. Stir in walnuts. Microwave on HIGH 3½ to 4½ minutes or until lightly browned, stirring every 2 minutes.

Raspberry Spinach Salad

CASHEW ORANGE SALAD

Toss the Cashew Dressing with the salad ingredients or arrange the salad and serve the dressing on the side—either way, you're in for a delightful taste sensation!

> **2 qts. torn red leaf lettuce**
> **2 qts. torn romaine**
> **3 oranges, peeled, sectioned**
>   **Cashew Dressing**
> **½ cup dry-roasted cashews**

- Toss together lettuce and oranges in large bowl. Serve with Cashew Dressing. Top with cashews.　　*8 servings*

CASHEW DRESSING

> **¼ cup dry-roasted cashews**
> **1 small garlic clove**
> **1 (8 oz.) container Light PHILADELPHIA BRAND Pasteurized Process Cream Cheese Product**
> **¼ cup plain yogurt**
> **1 tablespoon Dijon mustard**
>   **Dash of white pepper**

- Place cashews and garlic in food processor or blender container; process until finely chopped.
- Add remaining ingredients; process until well blended.

Prep time: 15 minutes

ABUNDANZA ZUCCHINI

This combination of zucchini and yellow squash with parmesan cheese will become a favorite main-dish accompaniment.

> **3 medium zucchini, cut into ½-inch diagonal slices**
> **2 yellow squash, cut into ½-inch diagonal slices**
> **1 medium red onion, cut into wedges**
> **2 tablespoons olive oil**
>   **Parmesan Sauce**

- Sauté vegetables in oil in large skillet 5 to 7 minutes or until crisp-tender.
- Serve with Parmesan Sauce.
  　　8 servings

PARMESAN SAUCE

> **1 (8 oz.) container PHILADELPHIA BRAND Soft Cream Cheese with Chives & Onion**
> **⅓ cup skim milk**
> **¼ cup (1 oz.) KRAFT 100% Grated Parmesan Cheese**
> **¼ teaspoon herb and spice blend seasoning**

- Stir together ingredients in small saucepan over low heat until smooth.

Prep time: 10 minutes
Cooking time: 7 minutes

MICROWAVE: • Combine vegetables and oil in 2-quart casserole; cover. Microwave on HIGH 9 to 10 minutes or until crisp-tender, stirring after 5 minutes. • Combine ingredients for Parmesan Sauce in 1-quart measure. Microwave on HIGH 2½ to 3 minutes or until thoroughly heated, stirring every minute. Serve with vegetables.

Microwave cooking time: 13 minutes

Abundansa Zucchini

RED BARON SLAW

Delicious on its own or as a topper for roast beef or corned beef sandwiches, this slaw is sure to please!

1 (8 oz.) container PHILADELPHIA BRAND Soft Cream Cheese
½ cup KRAFT Light Cholesterol Free Reduced Calorie Mayonnaise
2 tablespoons chopped onion
2 teaspoons cider vinegar
1 teaspoon sugar
½ teaspoon celery seed
½ teaspoon salt
¼ to ½ teaspoon cayenne pepper
3 cups shredded cabbage
3 cups shredded Chinese cabbage
½ cup green pepper strips

- Stir together all ingredients except cabbage and green peppers in large bowl until well blended. Add cabbage and green peppers; toss lightly. Chill.

12 servings

Prep time: 15 minutes plus chilling

Chinese cabbage is a mild-tasting vegetable. It has long, cylindrical, loosely packed leaves. To prepare, cut off exposed stem, slice cabbage in half and remove tough, wedge-shaped inner stem before shredding.

SALSA CORN CHOWDER

For a hearty entrée, add chopped cooked chicken or ham to this savory chowder. Serve with cornbread or tortillas.

1½ cups chopped onions
2 tablespoons PARKAY Margarine
1 tablespoon flour
1 tablespoon chili powder
1 teaspoon ground cumin
1 (16 oz.) pkg. BIRDS EYE Sweet Corn, thawed
2 cups salsa
1 (13¾ oz.) can chicken broth
1 (4 oz.) jar chopped pimento, drained
1 (8 oz.) container PHILADELPHIA BRAND Soft Cream Cheese
1 cup milk

- Sauté onions in margarine in large saucepan. Stir in flour and seasonings.
- Add corn, salsa, broth and pimento. Bring to boil; remove from heat.
- Gradually add ¼ cup hot mixture to cream cheese in small bowl, stirring until well blended.
- Add cream cheese mixture and milk to saucepan, stirring until well blended.
- Cook until thoroughly heated. *Do not boil.* Garnish individual servings with fresh cilantro, if desired.   *6 to 8 servings*

Prep time: 35 minutes

MICROWAVE: • Microwave onions and margarine in 3-quart casserole on HIGH 2 to 3 minutes or until onions are tender. • Stir in flour and seasonings. • Add salsa and broth; mix well. • Microwave on HIGH 8 to 10 minutes or until mixture begins to boil, stirring after 5 minutes. • Stir in corn and pimento. • Gradually add ¼ cup hot mixture to cream cheese in small bowl, stirring until well blended. • Add cream cheese mixture and milk to corn mixture. • Microwave on HIGH 12 to 17 minutes, or until thoroughly heated, stirring after 9 minutes. *Do not boil.* • Garnish individual servings with fresh cilantro, if desired.

Microwave cooking time: 30 minutes

86

Salsa Corn Chowder

BASIL CREAM VEGETABLE MEDLEY

Dress up frozen vegetables with this creamy sauce made of PHILLY Cream Cheese, parmesan cheese and seasonings.

  1 (16 oz.) bag BIRDS EYE Farm Fresh
      Broccoli, Cauliflower and Carrots
  ¼ cup cold water
  1 (8 oz.) container PHILADELPHIA
      BRAND Soft Cream Cheese
  ¼ cup milk
  ¼ cup (1 oz.) KRAFT 100% Grated
      Parmesan Cheese
  1 teaspoon dried basil leaves, crushed
  ¼ teaspoon garlic powder

- Place vegetables and water in medium saucepan. Bring water to boil; reduce heat to medium. Cover; simmer 1 minute. Drain.
- Add remaining ingredients. Stir until thoroughly heated. *3 cups*

Prep time: 15 minutes

MICROWAVE: • Omit cold water. Place vegetables in 2-quart casserole; cover. Microwave on HIGH 8 to 12 minutes or until vegetables are crisp-tender. • Add remaining ingredients. Microwave, uncovered, on HIGH 2 to 3 minutes or until thoroughly heated, stirring after 2 minutes.

Microwave cooking time: 15 minutes

MELON COOLER SALAD

A colorful fruit salad with a tangy citrus topping, this salad is great when served with muffins or nut bread for a light lunch.

  1 (8 oz.) pkg. Light PHILADELPHIA
      BRAND Neufchatel Cheese,
      softened
  ½ cup frozen lemonade or limeade
      concentrate, thawed
  4 cups assorted melon balls

- Place neufchatel cheese and lemonade concentrate in food processor or blender container; process until well blended.
- Spoon melon balls into parfait glasses or individual bowls; top with cream cheese mixture. *8 servings*

Prep time: 20 minutes

ASPARAGUS DIJON

Dijon mustard adds zip to this asparagus side dish.

  1 (8 oz.) container Light
      PHILADELPHIA BRAND
      Pasteurized Process Cream Cheese
      Product
  2 tablespoons lemon juice
  2 tablespoons skim milk
  1 tablespoon Dijon mustard
  1½ lbs. asparagus spears, cooked, chilled

- Place all ingredients except asparagus in food processor or blender container; process until well blended.
- Arrange asparagus on individual salad plates; pour cream cheese mixture over asparagus. *6 servings*

Prep time: 15 minutes plus chilling

90

Melon Cooler Salad

RISOTTO PRIMAVERA

1½ cups medium grain or Arborio rice
3 tablespoons olive oil
3 garlic cloves, minced
1 (46 oz.) can chicken broth
½ teaspoon dried oregano leaves, crushed
2 (3 oz.) pkgs. PHILADELPHIA BRAND Cream Cheese, cubed
1 (16 oz.) pkg. BIRDS EYE Farm Fresh Cauliflower, Baby Whole Carrots and Snow Pea Pods, thawed
1 (10 oz.) pkg. BIRDS EYE Broccoli Cuts, thawed
⅔ cup (2½ ozs.) KRAFT 100% Grated Parmesan Cheese

- Sauté rice in oil in large skillet over medium heat until lightly browned. Add garlic; cook 1 minute.
- Stir in 1 cup broth and oregano. Cook, uncovered, over medium-low heat until broth is almost absorbed. Gradually stir in remaining broth.
- Cook 40 to 50 minutes or until broth is almost absorbed and rice is tender.
- Add cream cheese, stirring until melted. Add remaining ingredients; heat thoroughly, stirring occasionally. Serve with additional parmesan cheese, if desired. *8 to 10 servings*

Prep time: 1 hour and 15 minutes

EXOTIC FRUIT SALAD

Exotic fruits are finding their way into grocery stores. Take advantage of their availability and serve this salad often.

1 qt. strawberries, sliced
1 papaya, peeled, sliced
4 kiwi, peeled, sliced
4 star fruit, sliced
1 cup raspberries
Lime Dressing

- Arrange fruit on serving platter. Serve with Lime Dressing. *8 servings*

LIME DRESSING
2 cups thawed COOL WHIP Whipped Topping
1 (8 oz.) container PHILADELPHIA BRAND Soft Cream Cheese with Strawberries
¼ cup lime juice
1 teaspoon grated lime peel

- Place ingredients in food processor or blender container; process until well blended.

Prep time: 20 minutes

92

93

EGGPLANT GRILLADE

This creamy dill sauce is a nice complement to the typically mild taste of eggplant.

2 medium eggplant, cut into 1-inch slices
Salt
Olive oil
Dill Sauce

- Prepare coals for grilling.
- Sprinkle eggplant with salt; drain in colander 30 minutes. Rinse with cold water; pat dry.
- Place foil brushed with oil on grill over hot coals (coals will be glowing). Puncture foil with fork.
- Brush eggplant slices with oil; place on foil. Grill, covered, 4 to 5 minutes on each side or until tender. Serve with Dill Sauce.

6 servings

DILL SAUCE
1 green onion, sliced
1 garlic clove
1 (8 oz.) container Light PHILADELPHIA BRAND Pasteurized Process Cream Cheese Product
3 tablespoons lemon juice
1 tablespoon olive oil
1 tablespoon fresh dill or ½ teaspoon dried dill weed
¼ teaspoon salt

- Place onions and garlic in food processor or blender container; process until finely chopped.
- Add remaining ingredients; process until well blended.

Prep time: 15 minutes
Cooking time: 10 minutes

TOMATOES WITH BASIL CREAM

Nothing is better than summer-ripe tomatoes—unless, of course, the tomatoes are topped with this creamy PHILLY Cream Cheese topping.

1 garlic clove
1 (8 oz.) container Light PHILADELPHIA BRAND Pasteurized Process Cream Cheese Product
2 tablespoons white wine vinegar
2 tablespoons chopped fresh basil or 1 teaspoon dried basil leaves, crushed
1 tablespoon chopped fresh parsley
½ teaspoon salt
¼ teaspoon pepper
2 red tomatoes, thinly sliced
2 yellow tomatoes, thinly sliced
1 tablespoon chopped fresh parsley

- Place garlic in food processor or blender container; process until finely chopped.
- Add cream cheese product, vinegar, basil, 1 tablespoon parsley, salt and pepper; process until well blended.
- Arrange tomatoes on serving platter. Spoon cream cheese mixture over tomatoes. Sprinkle with 1 tablespoon parsley. Garnish with fresh basil leaves, if desired.

10 servings

Prep time: 15 minutes

Variation: Substitute two additional red tomatoes for yellow tomatoes.

Yellow tomatoes taste sweeter than red varieties because of their higher sugar content. They are available mid to late summer, although some specialty producers grow them year round. Tomatoes are an excellent source of vitamins A and C.

Tomatoes with Basil Cream

OAXACAN CHILIES

6 Anaheim chilies or small green
   peppers
1⅓ cups MINUTE Rice, uncooked
1 (8 oz.) container PHILADELPHIA
   BRAND Soft Cream Cheese with
   Herb & Garlic
1 teaspoon chili power
½ teaspoon salt
½ cup (2 ozs.) KRAFT Shredded
   Monterey Jack Cheese
1 medium tomato, chopped
1 tablespoon chopped fresh cilantro
1 tablespoon lime juice

- Place chilies on broiler pan. Broil, turning
  frequently, until slightly charred. Cool
  slightly. Cut in half; remove seeds.
- Preheat oven to 350°.
- Prepare rice according to package
  directions.
- Mix together rice, cream cheese, chili
  powder and salt in medium bowl until well
  blended. Fill chilies with rice mixture;
  place in 12×8-inch baking dish.
- Bake 20 minutes. Sprinkle with monterey
  jack cheese; continue baking 5 minutes.
- Mix together tomatoes, cilantro and lime
  juice in small bowl. Serve with chilies.

6 servings

Prep time: 30 minutes
Cooking time: 25 minutes

MICROWAVE: • Prepare recipe as directed
except for baking. • Microwave on HIGH
8 to 12 minutes or until thoroughly heated,
turning dish after 5 minutes. • Sprinkle
with monterey jack cheese; microwave on
HIGH 1 minute. • Mix together tomatoes,
cilantro and lime juice in small bowl. Serve
with chilies.

Microwave cooking time: 13 minutes

Anaheim chilies are 6 to 7 inches long,
with a bright green color. These peppers
have a mild to slightly hot flavor.

CARIBBEAN FRUIT SALAD

1 (8 oz.) container PHILADELPHIA
   BRAND Soft Cream Cheese with
   Pineapple
½ cup pineapple juice
1 pt. strawberries, sliced
4 kiwi, peeled, sliced
2 oranges, peeled, sectioned
1 mango, peeled, cubed
1 star fruit, sliced
   Peeled cantaloupe slices
   Peeled honeydew melon slices
½ cup BAKER'S ANGEL FLAKE
   Coconut, toasted

- Stir together cream cheese and pineapple
  juice in small bowl until well blended;
  chill.
- Arrange fruit on individual salad plates.
  Top with cream cheese mixture. Sprinkle
  with coconut.   *8 servings*

Prep time: 20 minutes plus chilling

Mango is a tropical fruit with a delicate
floral fragrance and sweet flavor. It
should ripen at room temperature; it is
soft to the touch when ready to eat. To
peel, score the mango lengthwise and
remove a portion of the peel. There is a
large flat pit inside; pry the fruit slice
away from the pit. Repeat with remaining
fruit.

96

Caribbean Fruit Salad

CREAMED SPINACH CASSEROLE

PHILLY Soft Cream Cheese makes this dish extra creamy.

> 2 (10 ozs. each) pkgs. BIRDS EYE Chopped Spinach, thawed, well drained
> 2 (8 oz.) containers PHILADELPHIA BRAND Soft Cream Cheese
> 1 teaspoon lemon pepper seasoning
> ⅓ cup crushed seasoned croutons

- Preheat oven to 350°.
- Stir together all ingredients except croutons in medium bowl until well blended. Spoon into 1-quart casserole. Sprinkle with croutons.
- Bake 25 to 30 minutes or until thoroughly heated. *6 to 8 servings*

Prep time: 10 minutes
Cooking time: 30 minutes

MICROWAVE: • Stir together all ingredients except croutons in medium bowl until well blended. • Spoon into 1-quart casserole. Sprinkle with croutons. • Microwave on HIGH 8 to 10 minutes or until thoroughly heated, turning dish after 4 minutes.

Microwave cooking time: 10 minutes

TAFFY APPLE SALAD

> 1 (20 oz.) can crushed pineapple in unsweetened juice, undrained
> 1 (8 oz.) container PHILADELPHIA BRAND Soft Cream Cheese with Pineapple
> 1 (8 oz.) container COOL WHIP Whipped Topping, thawed
> 3 cups coarsely chopped apples
> 2 cups KRAFT Miniature Marshmallows
> 1½ cups dry-roasted peanuts

- Drain pineapple, reserving juice.
- Beat cream cheese and reserved juice in large mixing bowl at low speed with electric mixer until well blended. Stir in pineapple and remaining ingredients. Chill. *10 servings*

Prep time: 20 minutes plus chilling

FAR EAST SESAME VEGETABLES

PHILLY Cream Cheese with an Oriental flair—this colorful vegetable side dish can also be served as a lunchtime salad.

> 1 cup cold water
> 6 cups broccoli flowerets
> 1 cup diagonally sliced carrots
> ½ cup red pepper strips
> ½ cup julienne-cut yellow squash
> 2 tablespoons sesame seeds, toasted
> Ginger Dressing

- Bring water to boil in large saucepan. Add broccoli and carrots; return to boil. Boil 1 minute; rinse in cold water. Drain. Combine all vegetables in medium serving bowl.
- Sprinkle with sesame seeds. Serve with Ginger Dressing. *8 servings*

GINGER DRESSING

> 1 (8 oz.) container Light PHILADELPHIA BRAND Pasteurized Process Cream Cheese Product
> 2 tablespoons light soy sauce
> 1 tablespoon cold water
> 1 tablespoon olive oil
> 1 teaspoon chopped peeled fresh ginger root

- Place ingredients in food processor or blender container; process until well blended.

Prep time: 25 minutes

98

Far East Sesame Vegetables

ONION GRATINÉ

2 large onions, thinly sliced
¼ cup PARKAY Margarine
1 (8 oz.) pkg. Light PHILADELPHIA
   BRAND Neufchatel Cheese,
   softened
1 cup (4 ozs.) shredded KRAFT Light
   Naturals Reduced Fat Swiss Cheese
¼ cup BREAKSTONE'S LIGHT
   CHOICE Sour Half and Half
2 eggs, beaten
2 tablespoons brandy
1 teaspoon seasoned salt
½ cup seasoned croutons, crushed

- Preheat oven to 350°.
- Sauté onions in margarine in large skillet
  until tender.
- Mix together cheeses, sour half and half,
  eggs, brandy and salt in large bowl; stir in
  onions.
- Pour into lightly greased 9-inch square
  baking dish.
- Bake 45 to 50 minutes or until set.
  Sprinkle with croutons.   *8 servings*

Prep time: 20 minutes
Cooking time: 50 minutes

ORANGE SALAD WITH CINNAMON DRESSING

8 oranges, peeled, sliced
1 qt. torn assorted greens
   Cinnamon Dressing

- Arrange oranges and greens on individual
  salad plates. Serve with Cinnamon
  Dressing. Garnish with orange peel, if
  desired.   *8 servings*

CINNAMON DRESSING

1 (8 oz.) pkg. Light PHILADELPHIA
   BRAND Neufchatel Cheese,
   softened
⅓ cup orange juice
1 tablespoon honey
1½ teaspoons grated orange peel
½ teaspoon ground cinnamon

- Place ingredients in food processor or
  blender container; process until well
  blended.

Prep time: 20 minutes

COOL CUCUMBER SALAD

4 cucumbers, thinly sliced
½ small onion, thinly sliced
1 (8 oz.) container Light
   PHILADELPHIA BRAND
   Pasteurized Process Cream Cheese
   Product
¼ cup tarragon vinegar
1 teaspoon chopped fresh dill or ¼
   teaspoon dried dill weed
¼ teaspoon salt
¼ teaspoon pepper

- Mix together cucumbers and onions in
  large bowl.
- Place remaining ingredients in food
  processor or blender container; process
  until well blended. Add to vegetables; mix
  lightly. Chill.   *8 servings*

Prep time: 20 minutes plus chilling

Orange Salad with Cinnamon Dressing

OVERNIGHT VEGETABLE SALAD

A lovely layered salad for a potluck party, buffet dinner or barbecue.

  1 cup cold water
2½ cups cauliflowerets
  2 cups broccoli flowerets
1½ qts. torn iceberg lettuce
  1 lb. OSCAR MAYER Bacon Slices, crisply cooked, crumbled
  2 cups shredded carrots
  1 (8 oz.) container PHILADELPHIA BRAND Soft Cream Cheese with Chives & Onion
  1 (8 oz.) container BREAKSTONE'S Sour Cream
  ¼ cup milk
  ½ cup chopped green onion

- Bring water to boil in large saucepan. Add cauliflowerets and broccoli flowerets; return to boil. Boil 1 minute; rinse in cold water. Drain.
- Layer lettuce, caulifloweret mixture, bacon and carrots in 4-quart bowl.
- Stir together cream cheese, sour cream and milk until well blended. Spread over salad to seal. Top with onions.
- Cover; refrigerate overnight. Toss before serving.　　*8 to 10 servings*

Prep time: 30 minutes plus chilling

PUMPKIN GRATIN

  1 (8 oz.) container PHILADELPHIA BRAND Soft Cream Cheese
  2 tablespoons packed brown sugar
  1 (16 oz.) can pumpkin
  ½ teaspoon salt
  ¼ teaspoon ground nutmeg
  ⅛ teaspoon pepper
  ½ cup half and half
  4 eggs
  1 cup (4 ozs.) KRAFT Gourmet Shredded Swiss Cheese

- Preheat oven to 375°.
- Stir together cream cheese and sugar in large bowl until well blended. Add pumpkin, salt, nutmeg and pepper; mix well. Blend in half and half.
- Add eggs, one at a time, mixing well after each addition. Stir in ¾ cup Swiss cheese.
- Spoon mixture into greased 1-quart gratin dish or 8-inch square baking dish. Place dish in large baking pan. Place baking pan on oven rack; carefully pour boiling water into baking pan to 1-inch depth.
- Bake 45 to 50 minutes or until knife inserted in center comes out clean. Immediately sprinkle with remaining ¼ cup Swiss cheese.　　*8 to 10 servings*

Prep time: 15 minutes
Cooking time: 50 minutes

REUNION FRUIT SLAW

A slight twist to an ordinary cole slaw—great for barbecues and family get-togethers.

    1 (20 oz.) can pineapple tidbits in
        unsweetened juice, undrained
    1 (8 oz.) container PHILADELPHIA
        BRAND Soft Cream Cheese with
        Pineapple
    ½ teaspoon ground cinnamon
    8 cups shredded cabbage
    1 red apple, chopped
    1 green apple, chopped
    1 cup seedless red grapes, halved

- Drain pineapple, reserving 2 tablespoons juice.
- Stir together cream cheese, reserved juice and cinnamon in large bowl until well blended. Add remaining ingredients; toss lightly. Chill.   *8 servings*

Prep time: 20 minutes plus chilling

MONTEREY APPLE SALAD

Keep this salad on hand for a light lunch or snack. It's delicious with date bread or bran muffins!

    1 (8 oz.) container Light
        PHILADELPHIA BRAND
        Pasteurized Process Cream Cheese
        Product
    ¼ cup BREAKSTONE'S LIGHT
        CHOICE Sour Half and Half
    ¼ teaspoon ground cinnamon
    5 cups coarsely chopped apples
    ½ cup coarsely chopped pecans, toasted
    ½ cup raisins

- Mix together cream cheese product, sour half and half and cinnamon in large bowl until well blended. Stir in remaining ingredients.   *8 servings*

Prep time: 20 minutes

CRUNCHY COZUMEL CITRUS SALAD

    1 jicama, peeled, cut into thin strips
        (approx. 2 cups)
    2 large oranges, peeled, sectioned
    1 large grapefruit, peeled, sectioned
        Lettuce leaves
        Citrus Dressing
    ¼ cup chopped dry-roasted peanuts

- Arrange jicama and fruit on lettuce-covered serving platter or individual salad plates. Serve with Citrus Dressing. Sprinkle with peanuts.   *8 servings*

CITRUS DRESSING

    1 (8 oz.) container Light
        PHILADELPHIA BRAND
        Pasteurized Process Cream Cheese
        Product
    ⅓ cup lemon juice
    1 to 2 tablespoons honey
    1 teaspoon ground coriander
    1 teaspoon grated orange peel
    ¼ teaspoon salt

- Place ingredients in food processor or blender container; process until well blended.

Prep time: 30 minutes

◆◆◆

Jicama is a brown-skinned root vegetable (like a potato). Its white crunchy flesh is similar to that of a water chestnut and its mild flavor complements many dishes.

Quick Weekday Meals

HAM & CORN POT PIE

Create this creamy main dish pie in minutes with leftover ham, frozen corn and refrigerated pie crust. Delicious... and easy, too!

½ cup chopped onion
½ cup chopped red pepper
2 tablespoons PARKAY Margarine
¼ cup flour
2 teaspoons dry mustard
⅛ teaspoon black pepper
½ cup milk
2 cups ham cubes
1 (10 oz.) pkg. BIRDS EYE Sweet Corn, thawed
1 (8 oz.) pkg. PHILADELPHIA BRAND Cream Cheese, cubed
½ (15 oz.) pkg. refrigerated pie crusts (1 crust)

- Preheat oven to 350°.
- Sauté onions and red peppers in margarine in large saucepan until tender. Blend in flour, mustard and black pepper; cook 1 minute.
- Gradually add milk; cook, stirring constantly, until thickened.
- Stir in ham, corn and cream cheese until well blended. Spoon into 9-inch pie plate.
- Place pie crust over ham mixture; press crust under edge of pie plate to seal.
- Bake 30 to 35 minutes or until pastry is golden brown.   *6 to 8 servings*

Prep time: 25 minutes
Cooking time: 35 minutes

TORTELLINI PRIMAVERA

A great dish that takes only minutes to prepare—perfect for unexpected dinner guests.

1 cup mushroom slices
½ cup chopped onion
1 garlic clove, minced
2 tablespoons PARKAY Margarine
1 (10 oz.) pkg. BIRDS EYE Chopped Spinach, thawed, well drained
1 (8 oz.) container PHILADELPHIA BRAND Soft Cream Cheese
1 medium tomato, chopped
¼ cup milk
¼ cup (1 oz.) KRAFT 100% Grated Parmesan Cheese
1 teaspoon Italian seasoning
¼ teaspoon salt
¼ teaspoon pepper
8 to 9 ozs. fresh or frozen cheese-filled tortellini, cooked, drained

- Sauté mushrooms, onions and garlic in margarine in large skillet. Add all remaining ingredients except tortellini; mix well. Cook until mixture just begins to boil, stirring occasionally.
- Stir in tortellini; cook until thoroughly heated.   *4 servings*

Prep time: 20 minutes

105

Tortellini Primavera

SOUTHWEST FAJITAS

Fajitas have quickly risen in popularity. After tasting these, you'll know why.

1 (1 to 1½ lb.) flank steak
¼ cup olive oil
2 tablespoons lime juice
1 garlic clove, minced
1 teaspoon crushed red pepper
1 large onion, thinly sliced
1 tablespoon PARKAY Margarine
1 (8 oz.) pkg. Light PHILADELPHIA BRAND Neufchatel Cheese, cubed
3 tablespoons finely chopped fresh cilantro
1 tablespoon lime juice
8 (6-inch) flour tortillas
½ cup salsa

- Score steak on both sides. Marinate steak in combined oil, 2 tablespoons lime juice, garlic and red pepper in refrigerator at least 2 hours, turning once. Drain.
- Prepare coals for grilling.
- Separate onion into rings. Place onions and margarine in center of 25×12-inch piece of foil. Seal foil to form packet.
- Place steak and onion packet on greased grill over medium coals (coals will have slight glow). Grill, covered, 16 to 20 minutes or to desired doneness, turning steak over after 8 minutes.
- Stir together neufchatel cheese, cilantro and 1 tablespoon lime juice in small saucepan over low heat until smooth.
- Wrap tortillas in foil. Place on grill; warm 5 minutes.
- Carve steak across grain into thin slices with slanted knife.
- Spread approximately 2 tablespoons neufchatel cheese mixture over each tortilla. Place meat and salsa in center of each tortilla; roll up.   *8 servings*

Prep time: 15 minutes plus marinating
Cooking time: 25 minutes

BUFFET SALAD WITH BLUE CHEESE DRESSING

Arranged attractively on a large glass or ceramic platter, this gorgeous main-dish salad can be the focal point of a bountiful buffet.

1 (8 oz.) pkg. Light PHILADELPHIA BRAND Neufchatel Cheese, softened
1 (6 oz.) pkg. KRAFT Blue Cheese, crumbled
1 (8 oz.) bottle KRAFT "Zesty" Italian Dressing
3 Belgian endive
2 tablespoons lemon juice
2 qts. torn assorted greens
3 tomatoes, cut into wedges
2 green, yellow or orange peppers, cut into strips
2 cucumbers, thinly sliced
1 small red onion, cut into rings
¼ lb. pea pods, blanched
¾ lb. rare roast beef, thinly sliced, cut into julienne strips

- Place cheeses in food processor or blender container; process until smooth. Add dressing; process until blended.
- Separate endive leaves; toss with lemon juice. Place endive and greens on large platter; top with vegetables and meat. Serve with blue cheese dressing.
                                   10 to 12 servings

Prep time: 25 minutes

107

Buffet Salad with Blue Cheese Dressing

ENCHILADAS SUIZAS

This spicy meatless main dish with southwestern flair is sure to become a family favorite.

     1 (8 oz.) pkg. PHILADELPHIA
         BRAND Cream Cheese, softened
     ½ cup green onion slices
   1½ cups (6 ozs.) KRAFT Shredded
         Sharp Cheddar Cheese
   1½ cups (6 ozs.) KRAFT Shredded
         Monterey Jack Cheese
     2 (4 oz.) cans chopped green chilies,
         drained
     ½ teaspoon ground cumin
     3 eggs
   12 (6-inch) corn tortillas
       Oil
     2 (8 oz.) jars enchilada sauce
     1 (4¼ oz.) can chopped pitted ripe
         olives, drained

- Preheat oven to 350°.
- Beat 4 ounces cream cheese and onions in small mixing bowl at medium speed with electric mixer until well blended. Reserve for topping.
- Beat remaining cream cheese, 1¼ cups cheddar cheese, 1¼ cups monterey jack cheese, chilies and cumin in large mixing bowl at medium speed with electric mixer until well blended.
- Add eggs, one at a time, mixing well after each addition.
- Warm tortillas in lightly oiled skillet. Spoon 2 tablespoonfuls cheddar cheese mixture onto each tortilla; roll up.
- Place in 13×9-inch baking dish; top with enchilada sauce and remaining shredded cheeses.
- Bake 20 minutes or until thoroughly heated. Top with reserved cream cheese mixture and olives.   *6 servings*

Prep time: 25 minutes
Cooking time: 20 minutes

BACON, LETTUCE & TOMATO SALAD

A take off on the BLT sandwich—hold the toast!

     1 head leaf lettuce, torn
     4 large tomatoes, cut into wedges
     1 onion, thinly sliced
   10 OSCAR MAYER Bacon Slices,
         crisply cooked, crumbled
       Parsley Dressing

- Arrange salad ingredients on large serving platter. Serve with Parsley Dressing.
                                        8 servings

PARSLEY DRESSING
     ½ cup fresh parsley, stemmed
     1 garlic clove
     1 (8 oz.) pkg. PHILADELPHIA
         BRAND Cream Cheese, cubed
     ⅓ cup milk
     ¼ cup KRAFT Real Mayonnaise
     2 tablespoons cider vinegar
     ¼ teaspoon salt
     ⅛ teaspoon pepper

- Place parsley and garlic in food processor or blender container; process until finely chopped. Add remaining ingredients; process until well blended.

Prep time: 20 minutes

Enchiladas Suizas

CREAMY TURKEY OVER PASTRY SHELLS

¾ cup mushroom slices
2 tablespoons PARKAY Margarine
3 tablespoons flour
1 cup milk
3 tablespoons dry white wine
1 (8 oz.) container PHILADELPHIA
   BRAND Soft Cream Cheese with
   Chives & Onion
1½ cups cubed LOUIS RICH Oven
   Roasted Boneless Turkey Breast
2 tablespoons chopped fresh parsley
1 (10 oz.) pkg. puff pastry shells, baked
⅓ cup sliced almonds, toasted

- Sauté mushrooms in margarine in medium saucepan until mushrooms are tender. Blend in flour; cook 1 minute.
- Gradually add milk and wine; cook, stirring constantly, until thickened.
- Add cream cheese; stir until well blended. Add turkey and parsley; cook until thoroughly heated.
- Spoon ½ cup turkey mixture into each pastry shell. Sprinkle with almonds. Garnish with puff pastry cutouts, if desired (see Note).   *8 servings*

Prep time: 20 minutes

Variation: Add ½ cup diagonally-sliced carrots with mushrooms.

Note: To make puff pastry garnish, thaw one sheet frozen ready-to-bake puff pastry according to package directions; cut into decorative shapes as desired. Bake at 375°, 10 to 12 minutes or until golden brown.

MICROWAVE: • Microwave mushrooms and margarine in 2-quart casserole on HIGH 2 minutes. Blend in flour; microwave on HIGH 1 minute. • Gradually add milk and wine; microwave on HIGH 4 to 8 minutes or until thickened, stirring every 2 minutes. • Stir in cream cheese, turkey and parsley. Microwave on HIGH 3 to 5 minutes or until thoroughly heated. • Spoon ½ cup turkey mixture into each pastry shell. Sprinkle with almonds. Garnish with puff pastry cutouts, if desired (see Note).

Microwave cooking time: 16 minutes

◆ ◆ ◆

To toast almonds in the oven, spread almonds in a single layer on cookie sheet. Bake at 375°, 5 minutes, stirring almonds once or twice. Watch almonds carefully, since they can easily burn.

To toast almonds in the microwave, microwave 1 tablespoon PARKAY Margarine and almonds in 9-inch pie plate on HIGH 3½ to 4½ minutes or until light golden brown, stirring every 2 minutes. Let stand 5 minutes. (Almonds will continue to cook after they are removed from the microwave.)

MEDITERRANEAN HERO

Try this American favorite made special with an Italian accent.

6 French or Italian bread rolls, split
1 (8 oz.) container PHILADELPHIA
   BRAND Soft Cream Cheese with
   Herb & Garlic
1½ cups coarsely shredded red leaf or
   romaine lettuce
1½ lbs. rare roast beef, thinly sliced
¾ cup roasted red peppers, drained

- Spread rolls with cream cheese. Fill with remaining ingredients.   *6 servings*

Prep time: 15 minutes

110

Creamy Turkey over Pastry Shells

SOUP MESA VERDE

Serve this soup with cornbread for a simple supper.

　　2 lbs. zucchini, cut into 1-inch slices
　　2 (10¾ oz.) cans chicken broth
　　1 garlic clove, minced
　　1 teaspoon curry powder
　　1 (8 oz.) container PHILADELPHIA BRAND Soft Cream Cheese with Chives & Onion

• Bring zucchini, broth, garlic and curry powder to boil in 2-quart saucepan. Reduce heat; simmer 10 minutes or until zucchini is tender. Remove zucchini from saucepan, reserving broth in saucepan.
• Place zucchini and cream cheese in food processor or blender container; process until well blended.
• Add cream cheese mixture to reserved broth in saucepan. Heat thoroughly, stirring occasionally. Serve warm or at room temperature. Garnish with zucchini slices, chives and curry powder, if desired.
8 servings

Prep time: 15 minutes
Cooking time: 15 minutes

Variation: Omit garnish. Top with salsa.

PITA VEGGIE SANDWICH

　　1 (8 oz.) container PHILADELPHIA BRAND Soft Cream Cheese with Chives & Onion
　　½ cup RANCHER'S CHOICE Creamy Reduced Calorie Dressing
　　2 cups broccoli flowerets
　　1 cup mushroom slices
　　1 cup green pepper strips
　　½ cup shredded carrots
　　¼ cup sunflower seeds
　　4 pita bread rounds, cut in half
　　½ cup alfalfa sprouts

• Mix together cream cheese and dressing in medium bowl until well blended. Add broccoli, mushrooms, peppers, carrots and sunflower seeds; mix lightly.
• Fill each pita half with ½ cup vegetable mixture. Top with sprouts. *8 servings*

Prep time: 20 minutes

BISTRO CHICKEN SALAD

　　6 cups cubed cooked chicken
　　2 large peaches, pitted, peeled, coarsely chopped
　　1 cup celery slices
　　1 cup walnut halves, toasted
　　4 large peaches, pitted, peeled
　　1 (8 oz.) container PHILADELPHIA BRAND Soft Cream Cheese with Pineapple
　　½ teaspoon salt
　　¼ teaspoon ground coriander

• Mix together chicken, two chopped peaches, celery and walnuts in large bowl.
• Place four peaches in food processor or blender container; process until smooth.
• Add cream cheese, salt and coriander to peaches; process until well blended. Add to chicken mixture; toss lightly. Chill. Serve on lettuce-covered platter, if desired. *8 servings*

Prep time: 30 minutes plus chilling

◆ ◆ ◆

For moist cooked chicken, place bone-in or boneless chicken breast in a saucepan. Cover with canned chicken broth, a few peppercorns and a bay leaf. Bring broth to boil. Cover; simmer 35 to 40 minutes per pound or until tender. Drain; cool.

Soup Mesa Verde

OLÉ BURGERS

2 lbs. ground beef
1 tablespoon finely chopped fresh
    cilantro
1 teaspoon ground cumin
½ teaspoon salt
1 avocado, pitted, peeled, mashed
1 tablespoon lemon juice
1 (8 oz.) container Light
    PHILADELPHIA BRAND
    Pasteurized Process Cream Cheese
    Product
2 green onions, thinly sliced
1 pickled jalapeño pepper, finely
    chopped
8 hamburger buns
    Lettuce leaves
    Tomatoes

114

- Prepare coals for grilling.
- Mix together ground beef, cilantro, cumin
  and salt in medium bowl. Shape into
  sixteen patties.
- Stir together avocado and lemon juice in
  medium bowl. Add cream cheese product,
  onions and peppers; mix well.
- Spoon 1 tablespoon avocado mixture onto
  center of each of eight patties; spread to
  within ½ inch of edge. Top with remaining
  patties; seal edges securely. Reserve
  remaining avocado mixture for topping.
- Place patties on greased grill over hot
  coals (coals will be glowing). Grill,
  covered, 2 to 4 minutes on each side or
  until desired doneness.
- Fill each bun with lettuce, tomatoes and
  patties. Top with remaining avocado
  mixture.   *8 servings*

Prep time: 20 minutes
Cooking time: 8 minutes

SCALLOPS & VEGETABLES WITH CREAMY CHIVE & ONION SAUCE

2 cups mushroom slices
1 cup green pepper chunks
¼ cup shredded carrot
1 garlic clove, minced
2 tablespoons PARKAY Margarine
2 lbs. bay or sea scallops
1 tablespoon PARKAY Margarine
    Creamy Chive & Onion Sauce

- Sauté vegetables and garlic in
  2 tablespoons margarine in large skillet
  over high heat 3 minutes. Remove
  vegetables with slotted spoon. Reduce
  heat to low.
- Sauté scallops in 1 tablespoon margarine
  in same skillet over low heat 6 to
  8 minutes or until opaque; drain liquid.
  Add vegetables to scallops in skillet; stir
  over low heat 1 minute. Serve with
  Creamy Chive & Onion Sauce. Garnish
  with lemon wedges and fresh dill sprig, if
  desired.   *8 servings*

CREAMY CHIVE & ONION SAUCE

1 (8 oz.) container PHILADELPHIA
    BRAND Soft Cream Cheese with
    Chives & Onion
¼ cup lowfat buttermilk
1 tablespoon lemon juice

- Stir together ingredients in small
  saucepan over low heat until smooth.

Prep time: 15 minutes
Cooking time: 12 minutes

◆ ◆ ◆

*Sea scallops are harvested from the
waters of the Northern and Middle Atlan-
tic states. Bay scallops are smaller and
sweeter than sea scallops and are harvested from in-shore bays from New
England to the Gulf of Mexico.*

Scallops & Vegetables with Creamy Chive & Onion Sauce

TUNA CAKES WITH LEMON CAPER SAUCE

½ cup PHILADELPHIA BRAND Soft
    Cream Cheese
2 tablespoons Dijon mustard
2 (6½ oz.) cans white albacore tuna,
    drained, flaked
½ cup dry bread crumbs
3 tablespoons chopped pitted ripe
    olives
1 tablespoon finely chopped fresh dill
¼ cup flour
2 tablespoons cornmeal
    PARKAY Margarine
    Lemon Caper Sauce

- Stir together cream cheese and mustard in medium bowl until well blended. Add tuna, bread crumbs, olives and dill; mix lightly but thoroughly.
- Shape ¼ cup firmly packed tuna mixture into 2-inch patty; coat with combined flour and cornmeal. Repeat with remaining tuna and flour mixtures.
- Melt 2 tablespoons margarine in large skillet over medium heat. Brown patties in batches 3 to 5 minutes on each side or until golden brown on both sides, adding additional margarine as needed. Serve with Lemon Caper Sauce.   *4 servings*

LEMON CAPER SAUCE

1 (8 oz.) container PHILADELPHIA
    BRAND Soft Cream Cheese
2 teaspoons lemon juice
2 teaspoons capers
2 teaspoons chopped fresh dill

- Stir together ingredients in small bowl until well blended.

Prep time: 20 minutes
Cooking time: 20 minutes

CHICKEN SALAD BOMBAY

PHILLY Neufchatel Cheese makes a wonderful creamy base for a salad dressing. The orange juice and peel give this salad a fresh flavor.

6 cups cubed cooked chicken
2 (11 oz.) cans mandarin orange
    segments, drained
1 (8 oz.) can sliced water chestnuts,
    drained
1 cup pea pods
1 (8 oz.) pkg. Light PHILADELPHIA
    BRAND Neufchatel Cheese,
    softened
⅓ cup orange juice
2 teaspoons grated orange peel
1 teaspoon curry power
½ teaspoon salt
1 (5 oz.) can chow mein noodles

- Mix together chicken, oranges, water chestnuts and pea pods in large bowl.
- Place neufchatel cheese, orange juice, peel, curry powder and salt in food processor or blender container; process until well blended. Add to chicken mixture; toss lightly. Chill. Top with chow mein noodles just before serving.

        8 servings

Prep time: 25 minutes plus chilling

To make decorative pea pods, cut a small "V" into each end of pea pod using small scissors or sharp paring knife.

116

117

TEQUILA SHRIMP

Tequila gives this dish a special kick!

1 lb. cleaned medium shrimp,
    uncooked
1 green pepper, cut into 1½-inch
    chunks
1 red pepper, cut into 1½-inch chunks
1 yellow pepper, cut into 1½-inch
    chunks
1 medium onion, cut into quarters
¼ cup oil
1 tablespoon tequila
1 tablespoon lime juice
1 garlic clove, minced
    Tequila Sauce

• Prepare coals for grilling.
• Arrange shrimp, peppers and onions on
  skewers.
• Marinate kabobs in combined oil, tequila,
  lime juice and garlic in refrigerator at least
  30 minutes. Drain.
• Place kabobs on greased grill over hot
  coals (coals will be glowing). Grill,
  covered, 1 to 2 minutes on each side or
  until shrimp are pink. Serve with Tequila
  Sauce.   *6 servings*

TEQUILA SAUCE

1 (8 oz.) container Light
    PHILADELPHIA BRAND
    Pasteurized Process Cream Cheese
    Product
2 tablespoons tequila
2 tablespoons lime juice
2 teaspoons chopped fresh cilantro
2 teaspoons grated lime peel

• Stir together ingredients in small bowl
  until well blended.

Prep time: 30 minutes plus marinating
Cooking time: 4 minutes

118

*Shrimp are graded according to size.
Large shrimp have a grade of 15 or fewer
per pound. Medium shrimp grade 36
count per pound and small shrimp run
about 60 count per pound.*

CHICKEN FAJITAS

*Tortillas spread with PHILLY Soft Cream
Cheese with Herb & Garlic add a burst of
flavor to the chicken-vegetable filling of
these fajitas.*

4 (approx. 2 lbs.) boneless, skinless
    chicken breasts, cut into thin strips
2 tablespoons oil
1 green pepper, cut into strips
1 red pepper, cut into strips
1 small onion, sliced
2 garlic cloves, minced
1 tablespoon oil
1 (8 oz.) container PHILADELPHIA
    BRAND Soft Cream Cheese with
    Herb & Garlic
16 (6-inch) flour tortillas, warmed

• Sauté half of chicken in 2 tablespoons oil
  in large skillet; remove chicken, reserving
  oil in skillet. Sauté remaining chicken in
  reserved oil. Remove chicken from skillet;
  keep warm.
• Sauté peppers, onions and garlic in
  1 tablespoon oil in same skillet. Add to
  chicken; mix lightly.
• Spread approximately 1 tablespoon cream
  cheese onto each tortilla. Place ½ cup
  chicken mixture in center of each tortilla;
  roll up. Serve with salsa, if desired.
                                     8 servings

Prep time: 20 minutes
Cooking time: 15 minutes

Tequila Shrimp

CHICKEN TORTILLAS ON THE GRILL

Have a Mexican Fiesta—serve this dish along with Coronado Dip (see page 32).

4 (approx. 1½ lbs.) boneless skinless chicken breasts
¾ cup KRAFT "Zesty" Italian Reduced Calorie Dressing
1 (8 oz.) container PHILADELPHIA BRAND Soft Cream Cheese with Chives & Onion
8 (6-inch) flour tortillas
1 qt. shredded lettuce
2 avocados, peeled, pitted, sliced (optional)
1 cup salsa

• Marinate chicken in combined dressing and ¼ cup cream cheese in refrigerator at least 30 minutes; drain.
• Prepare coals for grilling.
• Place chicken on greased grill over hot coals (coals will be glowing). Grill, uncovered, 6 to 8 minutes on each side or until tender.
• Spread remaining cream cheese over tortillas. Place, cream cheese side up, on grill until softened and cream cheese is melted.
• Slice chicken into strips.
• Place lettuce, avocados, salsa and chicken on center of each tortilla; roll up.

4 servings

Prep time: 15 minutes plus marinating
Cooking time: 16 minutes

120

HERBED FRITTATA

1 cup zucchini slices
⅓ cup green onion slices
2 tablespoons PARKAY Margarine
1 (8 oz.) container PHILADELPHIA BRAND Soft Cream Cheese with Herb & Garlic
¼ cup milk
6 eggs, beaten
2 cups frozen Southern-style hash brown potatoes, thawed
¼ teaspoon salt
⅛ teaspoon pepper
1 cup (4 ozs.) KRAFT Shredded Colby/Monterey Jack Cheese

• Preheat oven to 350°.
• Sauté zucchini and onions in margarine in 10-inch ovenproof skillet until tender.
• Stir together cream cheese and milk in medium bowl until well blended. Add eggs, potatoes and seasonings; pour into skillet.
• Bake 25 to 30 minutes or until set. Immediately top with shredded cheese. Let stand 5 minutes. *8 servings*

Prep time: 10 minutes plus standing
Cooking time: 30 minutes

Variation: Add six OSCAR MAYER Bacon Slices, crisply cooked, crumbled, with potatoes.

MICROWAVE: • Microwave margarine in 8-inch square baking dish on HIGH 30 seconds to 1 minute or until melted. • Stir in zucchini, onions and potatoes. • Microwave on HIGH 3 to 4 minutes or until zucchini is tender, stirring after 2 minutes. • Stir together cream cheese and milk in medium bowl until well blended. Stir in eggs and seasonings. Pour into baking dish; cover. • Microwave on HIGH 12 to 14 minutes or until eggs are almost set, stirring after 4 minutes. • Immediately top with shredded cheese. Let stand 5 minutes.

Microwave cooking time: 19 minutes

Herbed Frittata

SALMON TORTELLINI

This creamy tortellini can be served as a main dish with a variety of colorful fresh vegetables or as an accompaniment for poultry or seafood.

1 (7 oz.) pkg. cheese tortellini, cooked, drained
1 (8 oz.) container PHILADELPHIA BRAND Soft Cream Cheese with Smoked Salmon
½ cup finely chopped cucumber
1 teaspoon dried dill weed or 2 teaspoons chopped fresh dill

- Lightly toss hot tortellini with remaining ingredients. Serve immediately.

6 to 8 servings

Prep time: 30 minutes

EGGPLANT BULGUR CASSEROLE

A meatless main dish and pleasant change from pasta or rice, bulgur wheat resembles brown rice and wild rice in flavor and texture.

1 cup bulgur wheat
½ cup chopped green pepper
¼ cup chopped onion
¼ cup PARKAY Margarine
4 cups cubed peeled eggplant
1 (15 oz.) can tomato sauce
1 (14½ oz.) can tomatoes, undrained, cut up
½ cup cold water
½ teaspoon dried oregano leaves, crushed
1 (8 oz.) pkg. PHILADELPHIA BRAND Cream Cheese, softened
1 egg
KRAFT 100% Grated Parmesan Cheese

- Preheat oven to 350°.
- Sauté bulgur wheat, peppers and onions in margarine in large skillet until vegetables are tender.
- Stir in eggplant, tomato sauce, tomatoes, water and oregano. Cover; simmer 15 to 20 minutes or until eggplant is tender, stirring occasionally.
- Beat cream cheese and egg in small mixing bowl at medium speed with electric mixer until well blended.
- Place half of vegetable mixture in 1½-quart baking dish or casserole; top with cream cheese mixture and remaining vegetable mixture. Cover.
- Bake 15 minutes. Remove cover; sprinkle with parmesan cheese. Continue baking 10 minutes or until thoroughly heated.

8 to 10 servings

Prep time: 30 minutes
Cooking time: 25 minutes

MICROWAVE: • Omit water. • Microwave bulgur, peppers and onions in margarine in 2-quart casserole on HIGH 4 to 5 minutes or until vegetables are tender, stirring after 3 minutes. • Stir in eggplant, tomato sauce, tomatoes and oregano; cover. • Microwave on HIGH 10 to 15 minutes or until eggplant is tender, stirring every 6 minutes. • Beat cream cheese and egg in small mixing bowl at medium speed with electric mixer until well blended. • Place half of vegetable mixture in 2-quart casserole; top with cream cheese mixture and remaining vegetable mixture. • Microwave on HIGH 7 to 9 minutes or until thoroughly heated. Sprinkle with parmesan cheese. Let stand 5 minutes.

Microwave cooking time: 29 minutes

━━━━━━━━━━━ ◆◆◆ ━━━━━━━━━━━

Bulgur, a parboiled cracked wheat, is used in Middle Eastern and Greek cuisine. It is a shelf-stable grain which comes in fine, medium and coarse textures. Like rice, it should be cooked in liquid until all of the liquid is absorbed.

122

Salmon Tortellini

CHICKEN TOSTADAS

    3 cups shredded cooked chicken
1½ cups salsa
    8 tostada shells
    1 (8 oz.) container Light
        PHILADELPHIA BRAND
        Pasteurized Process Cream Cheese
        Product
1½ cups shredded lettuce
    1 tomato, chopped
    1 (8 oz.) pkg. KRAFT Light Naturals
        Shredded Mild Reduced Fat
        Cheddar Cheese

• Toss chicken with salsa.
• Spread tostada shells with cream cheese
  product; top with chicken mixture,
  lettuce, tomatoes and cheese. Serve with
  additional salsa and jalapeño pepper
  slices, if desired.   *8 servings*

Prep time: 20 minutes

CREAM OF TURKEY WILD RICE SOUP

A great idea for using leftover turkey that's perfect as a satisfying lunch or entrée.

    1 cup cold water
    1 oz. dried mushrooms
    ¾ cup finely chopped celery
    ¾ cup finely chopped green pepper
    ¼ cup PARKAY Margarine
    ⅓ cup flour
    2 (13¾ oz.) cans chicken broth
    1 (8 oz.) container PHILADELPHIA
        BRAND Soft Cream Cheese with
        Chives & Onion
    ½ cup milk
    2 cups cooked wild rice
1½ cups LOUIS RICH Oven-Roasted
        Boneless Turkey Breast cubes
    3 tablespoons dry sherry

• Bring water to boil; pour over mushrooms
  in small bowl. Soak 30 minutes; drain.
  Chop.
• Sauté celery and peppers in margarine in
  large saucepan until tender. Blend in flour;
  cook 2 minutes. Gradually add broth;
  cook, stirring constantly, until slightly
  thickened.
• Stir in cream cheese and milk until well
  blended. Add rice, turkey, mushrooms and
  sherry; cook, stirring occasionally, until
  thoroughly heated. *(Do not boil.)*
                                      8 servings

Prep time: 30 minutes plus soaking

Variation: Omit water. Substitute
1 cup fresh mushroom slices for dried
mushrooms. Sauté mushrooms with celery
and pepper.

Wild rice, like other rice, is really the starchy seed grain of a water-grown grass. The rice grass grows wild in the northern United States and southern Canada.

125

BELLA PARTY SALAD

4 qts. torn romaine
1 lb. rare roast beef, cut into thin strips
1 red pepper, cut into strips
5 green onions, sliced
   Blue Cheese Dressing

- Toss together salad ingredients in large serving bowl. Garnish as desired. Top with Blue Cheese Dressing.   *10 servings*

BLUE CHEESE DRESSING

1 (8 oz.) pkg. Light PHILADELPHIA BRAND Neufchatel Cheese, softened
1 cup BREAKSTONE'S LIGHT CHOICE Sour Half and Half
3 drops hot pepper sauce
½ teaspoon salt
½ cup (2 ozs.) KRAFT Blue Cheese Crumbles

- Place all ingredients except blue cheese in food processor or blender container; process until well blended. Stir in blue cheese.

Prep time: 15 minutes

TURKEY PITA BURGER

2 lbs. ground turkey
½ cup chopped fresh parsley
2 garlic cloves, minced
½ teaspoon salt
½ teaspoon pepper
1 large onion, sliced
1 tablespoon PARKAY Margarine
4 pita bread rounds, cut in half
1 large tomato, sliced
   Curry Sauce

- Prepare coals for grilling.
- Mix together turkey, parsley, garlic, salt and pepper in large bowl until well blended; shape into eight patties, ½ inch thick.
- Place onion and margarine in center of 25×12-inch piece of foil. Seal foil to form packet.
- Place patties and onion packet on greased grill over hot coals (coals will be glowing). Grill, covered, 12 to 14 minutes or until done, turning patties over after 6 minutes.
- Fill each bread round with patty, onions and tomatoes. Top with Curry Sauce.
    8 servings

CURRY SAUCE

½ cup PHILADELPHIA BRAND Soft Cream Cheese with Herb & Garlic
½ cup plain yogurt
¼ teaspoon curry powder

- Stir together ingredients in small bowl until well blended.

Prep time: 15 minutes
Cooking time: 14 minutes

HAM AND CHEESE CASSEROLE

1 (10 oz.) pkg. BIRDS EYE Pasta Primavera Style Recipe Vegetables in a Seasoned Sauce, thawed
1 (8 oz.) pkg. PHILADELPHIA BRAND Cream Cheese, cubed
⅓ cup milk
1½ cups (¾ lb.) cubed ham
⅓ cup cheese-flavored crackers, crushed

- Preheat oven to 350°.
- Cook vegetable mixture, cream cheese and milk in medium saucepan over medium-high heat until cream cheese is melted, stirring occasionally. Stir in ham.
- Spoon into 1½-quart casserole; top with crackers. Bake 25 minutes.
    4 servings

Prep time: 20 minutes
Cooking time: 25 minutes

126

Bella Party Salad

CRUNCHY SALMON BAGEL

1 (15½ oz.) can salmon, drained, boned, flaked
1 (8 oz.) pkg. Light PHILADELPHIA BRAND Neufchatel Cheese, softened
½ cup KRAFT Light Cholesterol Free Reduced Calorie Mayonnaise
½ cup chopped dill pickle
½ cup green olive slices
1 tablespoon dill pickle juice
1 teaspoon pepper
4 LENDER'S Bagels, split, toasted

• Mix together all ingredients except bagels in medium bowl until well blended. Spread onto bagels.   *4 servings*

Prep time: 10 minutes

128

SUMMER SALAD IN A ROLL

1 (8 oz.) container PHILADELPHIA BRAND Soft Cream Cheese with Herb & Garlic
¼ cup KRAFT "Zesty" Italian Reduced Calorie Dressing
2 medium yellow squash, chopped
1 medium zucchini, chopped
1 red pepper, chopped
1 cup shredded lettuce
½ cup chopped fresh parsley
8 sesame French bread rolls

• Stir together ½ cup cream cheese and dressing in large bowl until well blended. Add vegetables, lettuce and parsley; mix well.
• Cut ½-inch slice from one end of roll; remove center, leaving ¼-inch shell.
• Spread remaining cream cheese inside rolls; fill with vegetable mixture.
              8 servings

Prep time: 30 minutes

CREAMY ORZO WITH PROSCIUTTO

This savory pasta can be served as a hearty side dish or as a main course for a light supper or luncheon.

2 garlic cloves, minced
2 tablespoons PARKAY Margarine
1 (8 oz.) pkg. PHILADELPHIA BRAND Cream Cheese, cubed
½ cup chicken broth
Dash of turmeric
1 (16 oz.) pkg. orzo, cooked, drained
1 (10 oz.) pkg. BIRDS EYE Deluxe Tender Tiny Peas, thawed, drained
3 ozs. thinly sliced prosciutto, cut into julienne strips
Salt and pepper

• Sauté garlic in margarine in large saucepan. Add cream cheese, broth and turmeric; stir over low heat until cream cheese is melted.
• Stir in orzo, peas and prosciutto; heat thoroughly, stirring occasionally. Season with salt and pepper to taste. Serve with parmesan cheese, if desired.
              8 to 10 servings

Prep time: 25 minutes

Tip: Recipe can be doubled for a main-dish meal.

Orzo is a tiny rice-shaped pasta. It is generally used as a soup pasta; however, Italian cooks also use this pasta in flavorful side dishes.

Creamy Orzo with Prosciutto

BUTTERNUT SQUASH SOUP

¼ cup celery slices
3 tablespoons chopped onion
2 tablespoons PARKAY Margarine
1 lb. peeled butternut squash, cubed
1¼ cups cold water
1 teaspoon instant chicken bouillon
¼ teaspoon dried marjoram leaves
⅛ teaspoon black pepper
1 (8 oz.) container PHILADELPHIA
   BRAND Soft Cream Cheese
¼ cup roasted red peppers, puréed

- Sauté celery and onions in margarine in large saucepan until vegetables are tender.
- Add all remaining ingredients except cream cheese and red peppers. Bring to boil; reduce heat to medium. Cover; simmer 15 to 20 minutes or until squash is tender.
- Place mixture in food processor or blender container; process until smooth. Add cream cheese; process until well blended.
- Spoon into serving bowls. Spoon approximately 1 tablespoon red pepper purée onto each serving. Pull wooden pick through purée making decorative design as desired. Garnish with fresh basil, if desired.   *Four 1-cup servings*

Prep time: 30 minutes

MICROWAVE: • Microwave celery and onions in margarine in 2-quart casserole on HIGH 4 to 5 minutes or until vegetables are tender. • Add all remaining ingredients except cream cheese and red peppers; cover. • Microwave on HIGH 15 to 17 minutes or until squash is tender. • Place mixture in food processor or blender container; process until smooth. Add cream cheese; process until well blended. • Spoon into serving bowls. Spoon approximately 1 tablespoon red pepper purée onto each serving. Pull wooden pick through purée making decorative design as desired. Garnish with fresh basil, if desired.

Microwave cooking time: 22 minutes

◆ ◆ ◆

Use a vegetable peeler to peel the butternut squash—it is easier than using a paring knife and not as much squash will be wasted.

TURKEY PASTA SALAD

7 ozs. shell macaroni, cooked, drained
2 cups LOUIS RICH Oven-Roasted
   Turkey Breast cubes
1 cup celery slices
½ cup chopped red pepper
2 tablespoons chopped fresh parsley
1 (8 oz.) container PHILADELPHIA
   BRAND Soft Cream Cheese with
   Chives & Onion
¾ cup BREAKSTONE'S Sour Cream
¼ cup milk
½ teaspoon dried basil leaves, crushed
   Salt and pepper
   Fresh spinach leaves

- Stir together macaroni, turkey, celery, red pepper and parsley in large bowl.
- Stir together cream cheese, sour cream, milk and basil in small bowl until well blended.
- Add cream cheese mixture to macaroni mixture; toss lightly. Season with salt and pepper to taste. Chill.
- Add additional milk just before serving, if desired. Serve on spinach-lined salad plates.   *8 servings*

Prep time: 30 minutes plus chilling

Butternut Squash Soup

FOUR–CHEESE LASAGNA ROLLS

Cream cheese, ricotta, parmesan and mozzarella are the four cheeses in this hearty meatless lasagna.

8 lasagna noodles
1 (15 oz.) container ricotta cheese
1 (8 oz.) pkg. PHILADELPHIA BRAND Cream Cheese, softened
½ cup (2 ozs.) KRAFT 100% Grated Parmesan Cheese
1 egg
2 tablespoons chopped fresh parsley
1 teaspoon salt
1 (15½ oz.) jar spaghetti sauce
1 cup (4 ozs.) KRAFT Shredded Low-Moisture Part-Skim Mozzarella Cheese

- Preheat oven to 350°.
- Cook lasagna noodles according to package directions. Drain, rinse and pat dry.
- Beat ricotta cheese, cream cheese, parmesan cheese, egg, parsley and salt in small mixing bowl at medium speed with electric mixer until well blended.
- Spread each noodle with ⅓ cup cheese mixture; roll up.
- Spoon ½ cup spaghetti sauce into 12×8-inch baking dish. Place lasagna rolls in dish; top with remaining sauce. Sprinkle with mozzarella cheese.
- Bake 35 to 40 minutes or until thoroughly heated.   *8 servings*

Prep time: 30 minutes
Cooking time: 40 minutes

MICROWAVE: • Prepare lasagna rolls as directed except for topping with mozzarella cheese and baking. • Microwave on HIGH 6 minutes, turning dish after 3 minutes. • Sprinkle with mozzarella cheese; microwave on HIGH 5 to 6 minutes or until thoroughly heated, turning dish after 3 minutes. Let stand 5 minutes before serving.

Microwave cooking time: 12 minutes

SALAD NIÇOISE

2 (6½ oz.) cans tuna in water, drained, flaked
8 new potatoes, cooked, chilled, sliced
½ lb. green beans, cooked, chilled
½ lb. yellow wax beans, cooked, chilled
8 radishes, sliced
Niçoise or pitted ripe olives
Torn assorted greens
Herb Dressing

- Arrange tuna, potatoes, beans, radishes, olives and greens on serving platter or individual salad plates. Serve with Herb Dressing.   *8 servings*

HERB DRESSING

¼ cup fresh basil leaves
1 tablespoon fresh parsley, stemmed
1 small shallot
1 (8 oz.) container Light PHILADELPHIA BRAND Pasteurized Process Cream Cheese Product
⅓ cup skim milk
3 tablespoons white wine vinegar
½ teaspoon salt
½ teaspoon pepper

- Place basil, parsley and shallot in food processor or blender container; process until chopped. Add remaining ingredients; process until well blended.

Prep time: 35 minutes

132

Salad Niçoise

GRILLED LAMB SHASHLYK WITH MINTED CREAM SAUCE

PHILLY Cream Cheese, yogurt and mint are a perfect blend of flavors to complement these grilled lamb kabobs.

2 lbs. lean lamb, cut into 1½-inch cubes
½ cup SEVEN SEAS VIVA Red Wine! Vinegar & Oil Reduced Calorie Dressing
1 green pepper, cut into 1-inch chunks
1 red pepper, cut into 1-inch chunks
1 yellow pepper, cut into 1-inch chunks
1 small red onion, cut into wedges
1 lemon, thinly sliced
Minted Cream Sauce

- Marinate lamb in dressing in refrigerator several hours or overnight. Drain, reserving marinade for basting.
- Prepare coals for grilling.
- Arrange lamb, vegetables and lemon on skewers. Place on greased grill over hot coals (coals will be glowing).
- Grill, uncovered, 4 to 6 minutes on each side or to desired doneness, brushing frequently with reserved marinade. Serve with Minted Cream Sauce.   *8 servings*

MINTED CREAM SAUCE

1 (8 oz.) container PHILADELPHIA BRAND Soft Cream Cheese
½ cup plain yogurt
2 tablespoons chopped fresh mint
1 garlic clove, minced
⅛ teaspoon black pepper

- Place ingredients in food processor or blender container; process until well blended.

Prep time: 20 minutes plus marinating
Cooking time: 12 minutes

134

Grilled Lamb Shashlyk with Minted Cream Sauce

BEEF TENDERLOIN EN CROUTE

You'll receive rave reviews when you serve this elegant entrée.

1 (3 to 4 lb.) beef tenderloin
½ lb. mushrooms, finely chopped
2 tablespoons PARKAY Margarine
1 (8 oz.) container PHILADELPHIA BRAND Soft Cream Cheese with Herb & Garlic
¼ cup seasoned dry bread crumbs
2 tablespoons Madeira wine
1 tablespoon chopped fresh chives
¼ teaspoon salt
1 (17¼ oz.) pkg. frozen ready-to-bake puff pastry sheets
1 egg, beaten
1 tablespoon cold water

- Preheat oven to 425°.
- Tie meat with string at 1-inch intervals, if necessary. Place meat on rack in baking pan.
- Roast 45 to 50 minutes or until meat thermometer registers 135°. Remove from oven; cool 30 minutes in refrigerator. Remove string.
- Sauté mushrooms in margarine in large skillet 10 minutes or until liquid evaporates, stirring occasionally.
- Add cream cheese, bread crumbs, wine, chives and salt; mix well. Cool.
- Thaw puff pastry sheets according to package directions.
- On lightly floured surface, overlap pastry sheets ½ inch to form 14×12-inch rectangle; press edges firmly together to seal. Trim length of pastry 2½ inches longer than length of meat.
- Place meat in center of pastry; spread mushroom mixture over top and sides of meat.
- Fold pastry over meat; press edges together to seal. Decorate top with pastry trimmings, if desired.
- Brush pastry with combined egg and water. Place meat in greased 15×10×1-inch jelly roll pan.
- Bake 20 to 25 minutes or until pastry is golden brown. Let stand 10 minutes before slicing to serve.   *8 to 10 servings*

Prep time: 1 hour plus chilling
Cooking time: 25 minutes

◆◆◆

The simplest and most accurate way to check for doneness in meat is to use a meat thermometer. The thermometer should be inserted into the thickest part of the meat, making sure not to touch any bone. It will register 140° for rare meat, 160° for medium. The temperature of the meat will rise 5° to 10° during standing, so for perfect doneness remove meat from the oven accordingly.

136

137

OVEN–BAKED FRENCH TOAST WITH CRANBERRY MAPLE SAUCE

A great make-ahead brunch idea. Prepare this recipe as directed except for baking. Cover and refrigerate overnight. Uncover, then bake as directed.

>   1 (8 oz.) pkg. PHILADELPHIA BRAND Cream Cheese, softened
>   ¾ cup sugar
>   ¼ cup PARKAY Margarine
>   2 teaspoons vanilla
>   1 teaspoon ground cinnamon
>   4 eggs
>   2½ cups milk
>   1 (1 lb.) French bread loaf, cut into 1½-inch slices
>   1 cup cranberries
>   Cranberry Maple Sauce

* Preheat oven to 350°.
* Beat cream cheese, sugar, margarine, vanilla and cinnamon in large mixing bowl at medium speed with electric mixer until well blended. Add eggs, one at a time, mixing well after each addition. Stir in milk.
* Pour cream cheese mixture over combined bread and cranberries in large bowl; toss lightly. Let stand 15 minutes, rearranging bread in bowl occasionally to moisten evenly.
* Arrange bread in rows in greased 13×9-inch baking pan. Pour remaining cream cheese mixture over bread.
* Bake 40 to 45 minutes or until golden brown. Serve with Cranberry Maple Sauce.   *10 to 12 servings*

CRANBERRY MAPLE SAUCE

>   1 cup LOG CABIN Syrup
>   2 cups cranberries
>   2 tablespoons sugar

* Bring syrup to boil in medium saucepan. Add cranberries and sugar.
* Cook over low heat 10 minutes, stirring occasionally. Cool slightly.

Prep time: 25 minutes plus standing
Cooking time: 45 minutes

LAKESIDE LOBSTER TAILS

PHILLY Cream Cheese blended with white wine and onions makes a simple but splendid topping for fresh lobster tails.

>   4 (1 lb. each) cleaned lobster tails with shells
>   Herb Wine Sauce

* Prepare coals for grilling.
* Cut each lobster tail through center of back with knife or kitchen shears; split open.
* Place lobster, shell side down, on greased grill over hot coals (coals will be glowing). Grill, covered, 5 to 8 minutes on each side or until shell is bright red and lobster meat is white.
* Serve with Herb Wine Sauce. Garnish with lemon wedges, if desired.
                    4 servings

HERB WINE SAUCE

>   1 (8 oz.) container PHILADELPHIA BRAND Soft Cream Cheese with Herb & Garlic
>   ¼ cup dry white wine
>   2 green onions, thinly sliced
>   ½ teaspoon salt

* Stir together ingredients in small bowl until well blended.

Prep time: 15 minutes
Cooking time: 16 minutes

138

139

CHICKEN RAGOUT WITH ORZO

⅔ cup chopped onion
1 (4 oz.) can mushrooms, drained
⅓ cup celery slices
⅓ cup finely chopped carrot
¼ lb. Italian sausage, casing removed, crumbled
4 OSCAR MAYER Bacon Slices, chopped
1 tablespoon olive oil
1½ lbs. boneless skinless chicken breasts, cut into ½-inch pieces
1 bay leaf
1 large garlic clove, minced
¾ cup dry Marsala wine
1 (14½ oz.) can tomatoes, cut up, undrained
1 cup chicken broth
⅛ teaspoon ground cloves
1 (8 oz.) container PHILADELPHIA BRAND Soft Cream Cheese with Olives & Pimento
¾ cup (4 ozs.) orzo, cooked, drained

- Sauté onions, mushrooms, celery, carrots, sausage and bacon in oil in Dutch oven 5 minutes.
- Add chicken, bay leaf and garlic; cook, stirring occasionally, 4 minutes.
- Add wine. Bring to boil; reduce heat to medium. Simmer 10 to 15 minutes or until only slight amount of liquid remains.
- Stir in tomatoes, broth and cloves. Bring to boil over medium-high heat; reduce heat to medium. Simmer 20 minutes or until slightly thickened. Remove from heat.
- Stir in cream cheese and orzo; mix well.

6 servings

Prep time: 30 minutes
Cooking time: 40 minutes

FETTUCCINE WITH SUN-DRIED TOMATO CREAM

⅔ cup sun-dried tomatoes
3 to 4 garlic cloves
1 (8 oz.) container PHILADELPHIA BRAND Soft Cream Cheese
½ teaspoon dried oregano leaves, crushed
¼ cup PARKAY Margarine
¼ cup BREAKSTONE'S Sour Cream
1 lb. fettuccine, cooked, drained
¼ cup olive oil
Salt and pepper
2 tablespoons chopped fresh parsley

- Cover tomatoes with boiling water; let stand 10 minutes. Drain.
- Place tomatoes and garlic in food processor or blender container; process until coarsely chopped. Add cream cheese and oregano; process until well blended.
- Melt margarine in medium saucepan; stir in cream cheese mixture and sour cream. Cook until thoroughly heated.
- Toss hot fettuccine with oil.
- Add cream cheese mixture. Season with salt and pepper to taste. Sprinkle with chopped parsley. Serve immediately.

8 to 10 servings

Prep time: 30 minutes

Sun-dried tomatoes can be purchased dried or packed in oil, usually olive oil. The dry-pack tomatoes, like good quality dried fruit, should be slightly moist to the touch.

Fettuccine with Sun-Dried Tomato Cream

GRILLED SALMON WITH CREAMY CUCUMBER SAUCE

6 to 8 salmon fillets, 1 to 1½ inches
    thick
¼ cup olive oil
2 tablespoons chopped fresh dill or
    1 teaspoon dried dill weed
1 tablespoon lime juice
    Creamy Cucumber Sauce

• Marinate salmon in combined oil, dill and lime juice in refrigerator at least 1 hour. Drain.
• Prepare coals for grilling.
• Place salmon on greased grill over hot coals (coals will be glowing). Grill, covered, 5 to 8 minutes on each side or until fish flakes easily with fork. Serve with Creamy Cucumber Sauce. Garnish with fresh dill sprig, if desired.

8 servings

CREAMY CUCUMBER SAUCE

1 (8 oz.) pkg. Light PHILADELPHIA
    BRAND Neufchatel Cheese,
    softened
3 tablespoons lime juice
3 tablespoons skim milk
2 tablespoons chopped fresh dill or
    1 teaspoon dried dill weed
¼ teaspoon salt
⅛ teaspoon pepper
1 cucumber, peeled, seeded, chopped

• Beat all ingredients except cucumber in small mixing bowl at medium speed with electric mixer until well blended. Stir in cucumber.

Prep time: 30 minutes plus marinating
Cooking time: 16 minutes

Note: For thinner sauce, increase skim milk by 1 to 2 tablespoons.

◆ ◆ ◆

Salmon and swordfish steaks are excellent types of fish for grilling because of their firm flesh. Lightly brush the surface of the fish and grill grate with vegetable oil to prevent sticking.

CORNBREAD–STUFFED TURKEY BREAST

PHILLY Soft Cream Cheese with Pineapple adds a hint of sweetness to this savory stuffing.

1 (3½ to 4 lb.) LOUIS RICH Fresh
    Turkey Breast Half
1 (8 oz.) container PHILADELPHIA
    BRAND Soft Cream Cheese with
    Pineapple
2 cups crumbled cornbread
1 egg, beaten
½ cup chopped onion
¼ cup chopped pecans, toasted
1½ teaspoons poultry seasoning

• Preheat oven to 325°.
• Rinse turkey; pat dry. Loosen skin with knife; pull back skin, leaving skin attached along one edge.
• Stir together remaining ingredients in medium bowl until well blended. Place mixture between meat and skin. Replace skin; secure with wooden picks. Place in roasting pan.
• Bake 1 hour to 1 hour and 30 minutes or until meat thermometer registers 160°, brushing occasionally with pan drippings. Let stand, covered, 15 minutes before slicing. Remove wooden picks.

8 servings

Prep time: 15 minutes plus standing
Cooking time: 1 hour and 30 minutes

142

143

HERB–CRUSTED PORK ROAST WITH APRICOT FILLING

This savory roast, seasoned with a variety of herbs, is made extra special with a creamy apricot filling.

1 (3½ to 4 lb.) center-cut boneless pork roast
1 (8 oz.) container PHILADELPHIA BRAND Soft Cream Cheese with Chives & Onion
1 cup chopped dried apricots
1 garlic clove, minced
2 teaspoons dried rosemary leaves, crushed
1 teaspoon dried thyme leaves, crushed
¾ teaspoon pepper
½ teaspoon salt
1 tablespoon oil
Gravy

- Preheat oven to 325°.
- Remove string from meat. Cut 2½-inch wide pocket through meat.
- Stir together cream cheese and apricots in small bowl until well blended; fill meat pocket with apricot mixture.
- Coat meat with combined garlic and seasonings; pat with oil. Place meat, fat side up, on rack in baking pan.
- Roast 1 hour to 1 hour and 30 minutes or until meat thermometer registers 165°. Let stand, covered, 10 to 15 minutes before slicing. (Temperature will rise 5° to 10° during standing.) Remove meat to platter, reserving ¼ cup pan drippings for Gravy. Keep meat warm. Serve with Gravy. *10 to 12 servings*

GRAVY

¼ cup reserved pan drippings
3 tablespoons flour
Cold water
¼ teaspoon salt
⅛ teaspoon pepper

- Pour drippings into small saucepan. Stir in flour. Cook over low heat, stirring constantly, until mixture comes to boil.
- Gradually stir in 1 cup water; cook, stirring constantly, until mixture boils and thickens.
- Add additional water, 1 tablespoon at a time, if necessary, to reach desired consistency. Stir in salt and pepper.

Prep time: 25 minutes plus standing
Cooking time: 1 hour and 30 minutes

A cooked mixture of fat and flour whisked together, otherwise known as roux, is the thickening element in many gravies and sauces. In this recipe, the fat comes from the pan drippings, giving the gravy a rich, delicious flavor. It is important to cook the roux slowly and evenly, whisking constantly, so as not to impart a burnt flavor to the gravy.

146

147

PASTA TOSSED WITH BLUE CHEESE SAUCE

A quick, yet elegant recipe using leftover ham.

>   1 cup coarsely chopped leeks
>   ¼ cup coarsely chopped pecans
>   2 tablespoons PARKAY Margarine
> 1½ cups ham strips
>   ¼ cup Madeira wine or chicken broth
>   1 garlic clove, minced
>   1 (8 oz.) container PHILADELPHIA
>   BRAND Soft Cream Cheese
>   2 tablespoons milk
>   ½ cup (2 ozs.) KRAFT Blue Cheese
>   Crumbles
>   8 ozs. fettuccine, cooked, drained

- Sauté leeks and pecans in margarine in medium skillet until leeks are tender. Add ham; cook until thoroughly heated.
- Cook wine and garlic in medium saucepan over low heat 1 minute. Add cream cheese and milk; stir until cream cheese is smooth. Remove from heat; stir in blue cheese.
- Toss all ingredients together. Serve immediately.   *4 servings*

Prep time: 15 minutes
Cooking time: 15 minutes

148

Variation: Substitute OSCAR MAYER Smoked Cooked Ham Slices, cut into strips, for ham strips.

MICROWAVE: • Place leeks, pecans and margarine in 1-quart casserole; cover.
• Microwave on HIGH 3 to 5 minutes or until leeks are tender, stirring after 2 minutes. Stir in ham. • Microwave on HIGH 2 to 3 minutes or until thoroughly heated. • Microwave wine and garlic in 1-quart bowl on HIGH 1 to 2 minutes or until hot. Stir in cream cheese and milk.
• Microwave on HIGH 2 to 3 minutes or until cream cheese is smooth, stirring every minute. Stir in blue cheese. Toss all ingredients together. Serve immediately.

Microwave cooking time: 13 minutes

--- ◆◆◆ ---

Leeks are a member of the onion family. Look for leeks that are 1 to 1½ inches in diameter. The base and white section of the leaves are the edible parts of the leek. Trim off root ends and all but 2 inches of the green tops before chopping. Wash carefully to remove sand.

149

BARBECUED SALSA TENDERLOIN

Pickled jalapeño peppers are available in most grocery stores. If unavailable, substitute a fresh jalapeño pepper.

3 (2 to 2½ lbs. total) pork tenderloins
1 (14½ oz.) can whole peeled tomatoes, undrained, coarsely chopped
1 small onion, chopped
3 green onions, thinly sliced
1 pickled jalapeño pepper, minced
¼ cup chopped fresh Italian parsley
¼ cup oil
2 tablespoons lime juice
1 garlic clove, minced
½ teaspoon black pepper
¼ teaspoon salt
1 (8 oz.) pkg. Light PHILADELPHIA BRAND Neufchatel Cheese, cubed

- Prepare coals for grilling.
- Marinate meat in combined remaining ingredients, except for neufchatel cheese, in refrigerator 30 minutes, turning meat occasionally. Drain, reserving marinade for sauce.
- Place meat on greased grill over medium coals (coals will have slight glow). Grill, covered, 45 to 55 minutes or until internal temperature reaches 170°, turning occasionally.
- Bring reserved marinade to boil in small saucepan; reduce heat to low. Add neufchatel cheese; stir until melted. Serve over meat. *8 servings*

Prep time: 30 minutes plus marinating
Cooking time: 55 minutes

◆◆◆

For a distinct smoky flavor, add hardwood chips to the white-hot charcoal fire. The varieties of hardwood chips available include cherry, hickory, apple, oak, pecan and mesquite. Of the varieties mentioned, mesquite produces the most intense smoky flavor. Never use softwoods, such as pine; softwoods impart an objectionable resinous flavor.

SWORDFISH WITH LEEK CREAM

Serve this entrée with fresh green beans and a tossed salad for a special dinner made easy.

4 (1 to 1½ lbs. total) swordfish steaks
2 tablespoons olive oil
Leek Cream

- Prepare coals for grilling.
- Brush fish with oil.
- Place fish on greased grill over hot coals (coals will be glowing). Grill, uncovered, 3 to 4 minutes on each side or until fish flakes easily with fork. Serve with Leek Cream. *4 servings*

LEEK CREAM

1 leek, cut into 1-inch strips
2 tablespoons PARKAY Margarine
1 (3 oz.) pkg. PHILADELPHIA BRAND Cream Cheese, cubed
3 tablespoons dry white wine
2 tablespoons chopped fresh parsley
½ teaspoon garlic salt
¼ teaspoon pepper

- Sauté leeks in margarine in medium skillet until tender. Add remaining ingredients; stir over low heat until cream cheese is melted.

Prep time: 15 minutes
Cooking time: 8 minutes

151

Swordfish with Leek Cream

SENSATIONAL SPINACH PIE

1 lb. Italian sausage, casing removed, cooked, crumbled
1 (15 oz.) container ricotta cheese
1 (10 oz.) pkg. BIRDS EYE Chopped Spinach, thawed, well drained
1 (8 oz.) container PHILADELPHIA BRAND Soft Cream Cheese with Herb & Garlic
1 cup (4 ozs.) KRAFT Shredded Low-Moisture Part-Skim Mozzarella Cheese
2 eggs, beaten
½ teaspoon hot pepper sauce
1 (15 oz.) pkg. refrigerated pie crusts (2 crusts)
1 egg, beaten

- Preheat oven to 400°.
- Mix together sausage, ricotta cheese, spinach, cream cheese, mozzarella cheese, two eggs and hot pepper sauce in large bowl until well blended.
- On lightly floured surface, roll out one pie crust to 12-inch circle.
- Place in 10-inch pie plate; fill with sausage mixture.
- Roll remaining pie crust to 12-inch circle; make decorative cutouts in pastry, if desired. Place pastry over filling. Seal and flute edges of pie. Decorate top with additional pastry; cut into decorative shapes, if desired. Brush with remaining egg.
- Bake 35 to 40 minutes or until pastry is light golden brown. Serve warm or at room temperature.   *10 servings*

Prep time: 20 minutes
Cooking time: 40 minutes

GRILLED TURKEY WITH WALNUT PESTO

1 (4 to 5½ lb.) turkey breast
Walnut Pesto Sauce

- Prepare coals for grilling.
- Place aluminum drip pan in center of charcoal grate under grilling rack. Arrange hot coals around drip pan.
- Place turkey on greased grill over hot coals (coals will be glowing). Grill, covered, 1½ to 2 hours or until internal temperature reaches 170°.
- Slice turkey; serve with Walnut Pesto Sauce. Garnish with red and yellow pear-shaped cherry tomatoes, fresh chives and basil leaves, if desired.   *12 servings*

WALNUT PESTO SAUCE

1 (8 oz.) container Light PHILADELPHIA BRAND Pasteurized Process Cream Cheese Product
1 (7 oz.) container refrigerated prepared pesto
½ cup finely chopped walnuts, toasted (see page 82 for directions)
⅓ cup milk
1 garlic clove, minced
⅛ teaspoon cayenne pepper

- Stir together all ingredients in small bowl until well blended. Serve chilled or at room temperature.

Prep time: 15 minutes
Cooking time: 2 hours

◆◆◆

For a beautiful presentation, place fresh basil leaves between the turkey skin and meat. Use fingers to gently lift skin from meat, starting at the V-shaped end. Place basil leaves under skin on each side of the breast. (Do not puncture skin.) Return skin to original position. Rub surface lightly with vegetable oil.

153

Grilled Turkey with Walnut Pesto

Dazzling Desserts

CHOCOLATE PEANUT BUTTER SQUARES

1½ cups chocolate-covered graham
    cracker crumbs (approx.
    17 crackers)
3 tablespoons PARKAY Margarine,
    melted
1 (8 oz.) pkg. PHILADELPHIA
    BRAND Cream Cheese, softened
½ cup chunk-style peanut butter
1 cup powdered sugar
¼ cup BAKER'S Semi-Sweet Real
    Chocolate Chips
1 teaspoon shortening

- Preheat oven to 350°.
- Stir together crumbs and margarine in small bowl. Press onto bottom of 9-inch square baking pan. Bake 10 minutes. Cool.
- Beat cream cheese, peanut butter and sugar in small mixing bowl at medium speed with electric mixer until well blended. Spread over crust.
- Melt chocolate chips with shortening in small saucepan over low heat, stirring until smooth. Drizzle over cream cheese mixture. Chill 6 hours or overnight. Cut into squares. *Approximately 1 dozen*

Prep time: 20 minutes plus chilling
Cooking time: 10 minutes

Microwave Tip: Microwave chocolate chips and shortening in small bowl on HIGH 1 to 2 minutes or until chocolate begins to melt, stirring every minute. Stir until chocolate is completely melted.

SPRING FLING FRUIT TART

1 cup flour
¼ cup packed brown sugar
½ cup PARKAY Margarine
1 (8 oz.) pkg. PHILADELPHIA
    BRAND Cream Cheese, softened
¼ cup granulated sugar
1 tablespoon grated orange peel
¾ cup whipping cream, whipped
    Peeled kiwi slices
    Strawberry halves

- Preheat oven to 350°.
- Stir together flour and brown sugar in medium bowl. Cut in margarine until mixture resembles coarse crumbs; knead mixture until well blended. Press onto bottom and ½ inch up sides of 10-inch tart pan with removable bottom.
- Bake 15 minutes or until golden brown. Cool.
- Beat cream cheese, granulated sugar and peel in large mixing bowl at medium speed with electric mixer until well blended. Fold in whipped cream; pour into crust. Chill until firm.
- Arrange fruit on top of tart just before serving. Carefully remove rim of pan.
10 to 12 servings

Prep time: 30 minutes plus chilling

Tip: When preparing crust, wet fingertips in cold water before pressing dough into pan.

154

155

ORANGE PEARLS IN CHOCOLATE SHELLS

The chocolate shells can be made in advance and, if well covered, stored for up to one week. The orange cream mixture can be prepared one day before serving. So relax... and enjoy the compliments!

> 1 (12 oz.) pkg. BAKER'S Semi-Sweet Real Chocolate Chips
> 1 tablespoon shortening
> 1 envelope unflavored gelatin
> ½ cup cold water
> 1 (8 oz.) container Light PHILADELPHIA BRAND Pasteurized Process Cream Cheese Product
> ¼ cup sugar or 6 packets sugar substitute
> ½ cup orange juice
> 1 teaspoon grated orange peel
> 2 cups thawed COOL WHIP Whipped Topping

- Cover outside of twelve seashells with foil, smoothing until tight.
- Melt chocolate chips with shortening in small saucepan over low heat, stirring until smooth.
- Spread chocolate mixture thinly over each foil-covered seashell with brush or small rubber spatula. Chill 10 minutes, keeping remaining chocolate mixture warm. Apply second coat of chocolate mixture. Chill until set.
- Remove chocolate-covered foil from seashells; carefully peel foil from chocolate. Cover chocolate shells; chill until ready to serve.
- Soften gelatin in water in small saucepan; stir over low heat until dissolved.
- Beat cream cheese product and sugar in large mixing bowl at medium speed with electric mixer until well blended. Stir in gelatin, orange juice and peel. Chill until thickened but not set.
- Beat cream cheese mixture until light and fluffy; fold in whipped topping.
- Spoon approximately ⅓ cup cream cheese mixture into each chocolate shell. Garnish with chocolate lace, orange segments and fresh mint leaf, if desired.

12 servings

Prep time: 1 hour plus chilling

Variation: Substitute twelve paper-lined muffin cups for seashells.

If chocolate shell cracks, brush crack with melted chocolate. Refrigerate until firm.

To make chocolate lace garnish, melt two (1 oz.) squares BAKER'S Semi-Sweet Chocolate with 1½ teaspoons shortening in small saucepan over low heat, stirring constantly until smooth. Cool slightly. Pour chocolate mixture into small squeeze bottle or pastry tube fitted with small writing tip. Pipe design onto waxed paper-lined cookie sheets. Refrigerate until set. Carefully peel waxed paper from chocolate design.

156

Orange Pearls in Chocolate Shells

CHOCOLATE HAZELNUT PEAR TORTE

Impress your friends and relatives with this European-style torte.

⅔ cup flour
2 tablespoons sugar
⅓ cup PARKAY Margarine
½ cup toasted, skinned, finely chopped hazelnuts
1 (8 oz.) pkg. PHILADELPHIA BRAND Cream Cheese, softened
¼ cup sugar
3 (1 oz.) squares BAKER'S Semi-Sweet Chocolate, melted, cooled
1 egg
1 (16 oz.) can pear halves, well drained
¼ cup toasted, skinned, coarsely chopped hazelnuts
1 (1 oz.) square BAKER'S Semi-Sweet Chocolate
1 tablespoon PARKAY Margarine

• Preheat oven to 375°.
• Mix together flour and 2 tablespoons sugar in medium bowl; cut in ⅓ cup margarine until mixture resembles coarse crumbs. Stir in ½ cup finely chopped hazelnuts. Press dough firmly onto bottom of 9-inch springform pan. Bake 10 minutes. Cool.
• Beat cream cheese and ¼ cup sugar in small mixing bowl at medium speed with electric mixer until well blended. Add three squares melted chocolate and egg; mix well. Spread evenly over crust.
• Arrange pear halves, cut sides down, over cream cheese layer. Sprinkle with ¼ cup coarsely chopped hazelnuts.
• Bake 25 minutes. Cool. Chill.
• Carefully remove rim of pan just before serving. Melt one square chocolate with 1 tablespoon margarine in small saucepan over low heat, stirring until smooth. Drizzle over torte. Garnish as desired.

10 to 12 servings

Prep time: 25 minutes plus chilling
Cooking time: 25 minutes

◆ ◆ ◆

To toast and skin hazelnuts, place hazelnuts in a single layer in shallow baking pan. Bake at 350°, 10 to 15 minutes or until golden brown. Immediately rub off skins with cloth towel.

STRAWBERRY COOKIE TARTS

These tasty treats are best eaten the day they are made.

1 (20 oz.) pkg. refrigerated sliceable sugar cookie dough
2 (8 oz.) containers PHILADELPHIA BRAND Soft Cream Cheese with Strawberries
¼ cup powdered sugar
¼ cup BAKER'S Semi-Sweet Real Chocolate Chips
1 teaspoon shortening

• Preheat oven to 325°.
• Slice cookie dough into thirty-six ¼-inch slices. Place on bottom and ¼ inch up sides of well-greased medium-size muffin pan.
• Bake 12 to 15 minutes or until edges are golden brown. Cool 5 minutes; remove from pan. Cool completely.
• Stir together cream cheese and sugar in medium bowl until well blended. Spoon into tarts.
• Melt chocolate chips with shortening in small saucepan over low heat, stirring until smooth. Drizzle over cream cheese mixture.

3 dozen

Prep time: 25 minutes
Cooking time: 15 minutes

Variation: Spoon cream cheese mixture into pastry bag fitted with large star tip. Pipe mixture into tarts.

158

Chocolate Hazelnut Pear Torte

GINGER CHEESECAKE ROULADE

What makes this cake so unique is its one-step method of preparing cake and filling together!

  1 (12 oz.) container PHILADELPHIA
      BRAND Soft Cream Cheese
  ½ cup granulated sugar
  2 tablespoons milk
  5 eggs
  ⅓ cup light molasses
  ¼ cup granulated sugar
  ¾ cup flour
  1 teaspoon CALUMET Baking Powder
  ½ teaspoon ground ginger
  ¼ teaspoon salt
      Powdered sugar

- Preheat oven to 375°.
- Grease 15×10×1-inch jelly roll pan. Line with waxed paper; grease paper.
- Beat cream cheese, ½ cup granulated sugar and milk in small mixing bowl at medium speed with electric mixer until well blended. Add two eggs, one at a time, mixing well after each addition. Pour into prepared pan.
- Beat three eggs in large mixing bowl at high speed with electric mixer 5 minutes or until thick and lemon colored. Gradually add molasses and ¼ cup granulated sugar; beat until well blended. Fold in combined flour, baking powder, ginger and salt. Pour over cream cheese mixture.
- Bake 15 minutes. Loosen sides from pan immediately; invert onto towel sprinkled with powdered sugar.
- Carefully remove waxed paper. Roll up cake with towel, starting at short side; cool on rack.
- Unroll; remove towel. Roll up. Sprinkle with powdered sugar, if desired.

10 servings

Prep time: 20 minutes plus cooling
Cooking time: 15 minutes

LEMON NUT BARS

  1⅓ cups flour
  ½ cup packed brown sugar
  ¼ cup granulated sugar
  ¾ cup PARKAY Margarine
  1 cup old-fashioned or quick oats, uncooked
  ½ cup chopped nuts
  1 (8 oz.) pkg. PHILADELPHIA
      BRAND Cream Cheese, softened
  1 egg
  3 tablespoons lemon juice
  1 tablespoon grated lemon peel

- Preheat oven to 350°.
- Stir together flour and sugars in medium bowl. Cut in margarine until mixture resembles coarse crumbs. Stir in oats and nuts.
- Reserve 1 cup crumb mixture; press remaining crumb mixture onto bottom of greased 13×9-inch baking pan. Bake 15 minutes.
- Beat cream cheese, egg, juice and peel in small mixing bowl at medium speed with electric mixer until well blended. Pour over crust; sprinkle with reserved crumb mixture.
- Bake 25 minutes. Cool; cut into bars.

Approximately 3 dozen

Prep time: 30 minutes
Cooking time: 25 minutes

160

Lemon Nut Bars

FRUIT COBBLER

Quick and easy, this cobbler is made from convenient ingredients and can be baked in a skillet.

1 (21 oz.) can cherry pie filling
1 (17 oz.) can fruit cocktail in heavy
    syrup, undrained
¼ teaspoon almond extract
1 (3 oz.) pkg. PHILADELPHIA
    BRAND Cream Cheese, softened
½ cup sugar
⅓ cup PARKAY Margarine, melted
2 cups variety baking mix
1 tablespoon sugar
½ teaspoon ground cinnamon
    Honey Cream Cheese

- Preheat oven to 375°.
- Mix pie filling, fruit cocktail and extract; pour into 2-quart casserole or 10-inch cast-iron skillet.
- Mix cream cheese and ½ cup sugar until well blended; gradually stir in margarine. Stir in baking mix.
- Crumble cream cheese mixture over fruit mixture. Sprinkle with combined 1 tablespoon sugar and cinnamon.
- Bake 35 to 40 minutes or until golden brown. Serve warm with Honey Cream Cheese.   *8 to 10 servings*

HONEY CREAM CHEESE

1 (8 oz.) pkg. PHILADELPHIA
    BRAND Cream Cheese, softened
2 tablespoons honey
1 tablespoon rum or orange juice
¼ teaspoon ground nutmeg

- Mix cream cheese, honey, rum and nutmeg until well blended.

Prep time: 15 minutes
Cooking time: 40 minutes

APPLE CREAM CRUMBLE PIE

PHILLY Cream Cheese adds a rich creamy layer to this apple pie.

½ (15 oz.) pkg. refrigerated pie crusts
    (1 crust)
1 (8 oz.) pkg. PHILADELPHIA
    BRAND Cream Cheese, softened
⅓ cup sugar
1 teaspoon vanilla
1 egg
⅔ cup BREAKSTONE'S Sour Cream
3 apples, sliced
½ cup flour
¼ cup sugar
1 teaspoon ground cinnamon
⅓ cup PARKAY Margarine
½ cup chopped pecans

- Preheat oven to 350°.
- On lightly floured surface, roll pastry to 12-inch circle. Place in 10-inch quiche dish or tart pan with removable bottom. Trim edges of pastry even with top of dish. Prick bottom and sides of pastry with fork. Bake 15 minutes.
- Beat cream cheese, ⅓ cup sugar and vanilla in large mixing bowl at medium speed with electric mixer until well blended. Add egg; mix well. Blend in sour cream. Pour into crust. Top with apples.
- Mix together flour, ¼ cup sugar and cinnamon in medium bowl; cut in margarine until mixture resembles coarse crumbs. Stir in pecans; sprinkle over apples.
- Bake 50 minutes. Cool. Garnish with cinnamon sticks tied with orange peel, if desired.   *12 servings*

Prep time: 30 minutes
Cooking time: 50 minutes

163

GREEK HONEY–CREAM TORTE

Definitely a dessert for nut lovers.

¼ cup coarsely chopped blanched
    almonds
¼ cup coarsely chopped salted cashews
¼ cup coarsely chopped pistachio nuts
¼ cup honey
1 (8 oz.) pkg. PHILADELPHIA
    BRAND Cream Cheese, softened
1 cup thawed COOL WHIP Whipped
    Topping
1 (10¾ oz.) frozen pound cake, thawed
    Coffee Frosting

- Preheat oven to 325°.
- Place nuts in shallow baking pan. Bake
  10 minutes or until lightly toasted, stirring
  occasionally. Cool completely.
- Beat honey in small mixing bowl at high
  speed with electric mixer 2 minutes or
  until thickened. Add cream cheese; mix at
  medium speed until well blended.
- Fold in whipped topping and nuts.
- Split cake lengthwise into three layers.
  Spread two layers with cream cheese
  mixture; stack. Top with remaining layer.
  Frost with Coffee Frosting. Chill.

12 servings

COFFEE FROSTING

4 ozs. PHILADELPHIA BRAND Cream
    Cheese, softened
2 tablespoons PARKAY Margarine
2¼ cups powdered sugar
1 teaspoon MAXWELL HOUSE Instant
    Coffee Granules

- Beat cream cheese and margarine in small
  mixing bowl at medium speed with
  electric mixer until well blended.
- Gradually add sugar, mixing until well
  blended. Blend in coffee granules.

Prep time: 20 minutes plus chilling
Cooking time: 10 minutes

BANANA BERRY BROWNIE PIZZA

*A fresh fruit pizza with a brownie crust
is a guaranteed success at any party.*

⅓ cup cold water
1 (15 oz.) pkg. brownie mix
¼ cup oil
1 egg
1 (8 oz.) pkg. PHILADELPHIA
    BRAND Cream Cheese, softened
¼ cup sugar
1 egg
1 teaspoon vanilla
    Strawberry slices
    Banana slices
2 (1 oz.) squares BAKER'S Semi-Sweet
    Chocolate, melted

- Preheat oven to 350°.
- Bring water to boil.
- Mix together brownie mix, water, oil and
  one egg in large bowl until well blended.
- Pour into greased and floured 12-inch
  pizza pan.
- Bake 25 minutes.
- Beat cream cheese, sugar, remaining egg
  and vanilla in small mixing bowl at
  medium speed with electric mixer until
  well blended. Pour over crust.
- Continue baking 15 minutes. Cool. Top
  with fruit; drizzle with chocolate. Garnish
  with mint leaves, if desired.

10 to 12 servings

Prep time: 35 minutes
Cooking time: 40 minutes

Microwave Tip: To melt chocolate, place
unwrapped chocolate squares in small bowl.
Microwave on HIGH 1 to 2 minutes or until
almost melted. Stir until chocolate is
completely melted.

164

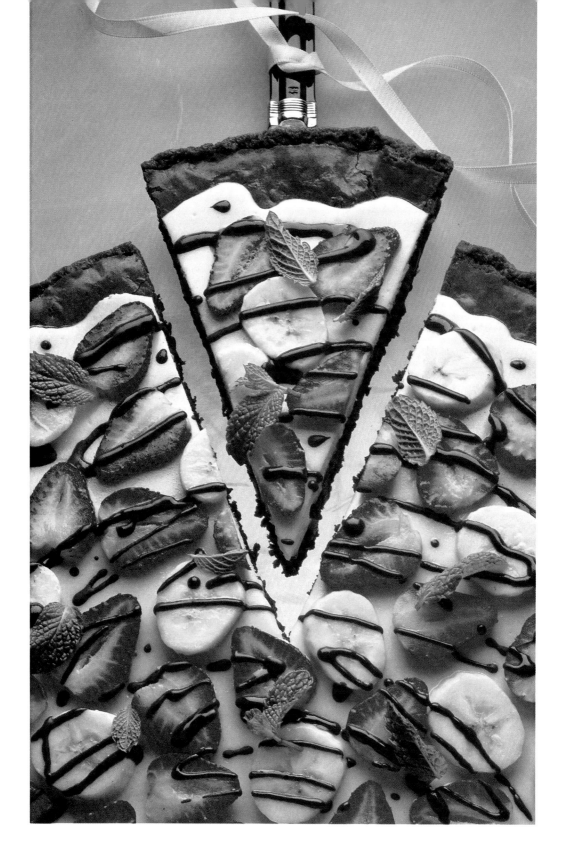

Banana Berry Brownie Pizza

WHITE MOUSSE WITH RASPBERRY SAUCE

This dessert can be made especially elegant when served as individual molded desserts.

½ cup milk
1 cup (8 ozs.) ready-to-spread vanilla frosting
1 envelope unflavored gelatin
¼ cup milk
1 (12 oz.) container PHILADELPHIA BRAND Soft Cream Cheese
2 teaspoons vanilla
2 egg whites, room temperature
¼ teaspoon salt
½ cup whipping cream
   Raspberry Sauce

- Mix together ½ cup milk and frosting in medium saucepan over low heat, stirring constantly. Remove from heat.
- Soften gelatin in ¼ cup milk in small saucepan; stir over low heat until dissolved. Add to frosting mixture; cool.
- Beat cream cheese and vanilla in large mixing bowl at medium speed with electric mixer until well blended. Blend in frosting mixture.
- Beat egg whites and salt in small mixing bowl at high speed with electric mixer until stiff peaks form. In separate bowl, beat whipping cream at high speed with electric mixer until stiff peaks form.
- Fold egg whites and whipped cream into cream cheese mixture.
- Pour into lightly oiled 1½- to 2-quart mold; chill until firm. Unmold; serve with Raspberry Sauce.   *14 to 16 servings*

RASPBERRY SAUCE
   1 (10 oz.) pkg. BIRDS EYE Quick Thaw Red Raspberries in a Lite Syrup, thawed
   ½ cup KRAFT Red Currant Jelly
   4 teaspoons cornstarch

- Place raspberries and jelly in food processor or blender container; process until well blended. Strain.
- Stir together cornstarch and raspberry mixture in small saucepan until smooth.
- Bring to boil over medium heat, stirring constantly. Cook until thickened, stirring constantly. Cool.

Prep time: 25 minutes plus chilling
Cooking time: 10 minutes

Microwave Tip: To dissolve gelatin, soften gelatin in milk. Microwave on HIGH 30 to 45 seconds or until dissolved, stirring every 15 seconds.

WALNUT SHORTBREAD BARS

1 (8 oz.) pkg. PHILADELPHIA BRAND Cream Cheese, softened
1 cup PARKAY Margarine
¾ cup granulated sugar
¾ cup packed brown sugar
1 egg
1 teaspoon vanilla
2½ cups flour
1 teaspoon CALUMET Baking Powder
½ teaspoon salt
¾ cup chopped walnuts

- Preheat oven to 350°.
- Beat cream cheese, margarine and sugars in large mixing bowl at medium speed with electric mixer until well blended. Blend in egg and vanilla.
- Add combined dry ingredients; mix well. Stir in walnuts. Spread into greased 15×10×1-inch jelly roll pan.
- Bake 20 to 25 minutes or until lightly browned. Cool. Sprinkle with powdered sugar just before serving, if desired. Cut into bars.   *Approximately 5 dozen*

Prep time: 15 minutes
Cooking time: 25 minutes

White Mousse with Raspberry Sauce

BLUEBERRY PEAR CREAM CHEESE CRISP

A perfect dessert for a crowd.

   2 cups old-fashioned or quick oats, uncooked
   1 cup flour
   ⅓ cup granulated sugar
   ⅓ cup packed brown sugar
   ½ cup PARKAY Margarine, melted
   2 (8 oz.) containers Light PHILADELPHIA BRAND Pasteurized Process Cream Cheese Product
   ½ cup granulated sugar
   2 eggs
   2 tablespoons lemon juice
   1 tablespoon grated lemon peel
   2 pears, peeled, cored, sliced, halved
   1 pt. blueberries

- Preheat oven to 325°.
- Mix together oats, flour, ⅓ cup granulated sugar and brown sugar in medium bowl until well blended. Stir in margarine.
- Reserve 1 cup oat mixture for topping. Press remaining oat mixture onto bottom of 13×9-inch baking pan. Bake 10 minutes.
- Beat cream cheese product and ½ cup granulated sugar in large mixing bowl at medium speed with electric mixer until well blended. Add eggs, one at a time, mixing well after each addition. Blend in lemon juice and peel; pour over crust.
- Layer pears evenly over cream cheese mixture; top with blueberries. Sprinkle reserved oat mixture over fruit.
- Bake 45 minutes. Serve warm with vanilla ice cream, if desired.   *16 servings*

Prep time: 20 minutes
Cooking time: 45 minutes

ORANGE POPPY SEED CAKE

   1 (8 oz.) container Light PHILADELPHIA BRAND Pasteurized Process Cream Cheese Product
   ½ cup PARKAY Margarine
   1 cup granulated sugar
   3 eggs, separated
   2 cups flour
   1 teaspoon CALUMET Baking Powder
   1 teaspoon baking soda
   1 cup BREAKSTONE'S LIGHT CHOICE Sour Half and Half
   2 tablespoons poppy seeds
   1 tablespoon grated orange peel
   ½ cup granulated sugar
   ⅓ cup orange-flavored liqueur
   ¼ cup orange juice
   3 tablespoons powdered sugar

- Preheat oven to 350°.
- Beat cream cheese product, margarine and 1 cup granulated sugar in large mixing bowl at medium speed with electric mixer until well blended. Beat in egg yolks.
- Mix together flour, baking powder and soda; add to cream cheese mixture alternately with sour half and half. Stir in poppy seeds and peel.
- Beat egg whites in small mixing bowl at high speed with electric mixer until stiff peaks form; fold into cream cheese mixture. Pour into greased 10-inch fluted tube pan.
- Bake 50 minutes.
- Stir together ½ cup sugar, liqueur and orange juice in saucepan over low heat until sugar dissolves.
- Prick hot cake several times with fork. Pour syrup over cake; cool 10 minutes. Invert onto serving plate. Cool completely. Sprinkle with powdered sugar just before serving. Garnish with quartered orange slices, if desired.   *16 servings*

Prep time: 30 minutes
Cooking time: 50 minutes

Variation: Omit orange-flavored liqueur. Increase orange juice to ½ cup.

Orange Poppy Seed Cake

STRAWBERRIES ELEGANTE

6 cups strawberry slices
2 tablespoons orange-flavored liqueur
or orange juice
1 (8 oz.) container Light
PHILADELPHIA BRAND
Pasteurized Process Cream Cheese
Product
3 tablespoons packed brown sugar
1 tablespoon orange-flavored liqueur or
orange juice
1 tablespoon skim milk

• Toss strawberries with 2 tablespoons
  liqueur in small bowl.
• Place cream cheese product, sugar,
  1 tablespoon liqueur and milk in food
  processor or blender container; process
  until well blended. Serve over
  strawberries. Garnish with fresh mint
  leaves, if desired.   *6 servings*

Prep time: 20 minutes

SPECTACULAR CANNOLIS

These cookies only look time-consuming!
With the proper pastry tip, filling the
cookies with PHILLY Soft Cream Cheese
with Strawberries is a snap!

1 (8 oz.) container PHILADELPHIA
BRAND Soft Cream Cheese with
Strawberries
2 tablespoons milk
2 (5½ oz.) boxes pirouette cookies
¾ cup BAKER'S Semi-Sweet Real
Chocolate Chips

• Blend cream cheese and milk in small
  bowl until smooth.
• Spoon cream cheese mixture into pastry
  bag; pipe into cookies. Chill 10 minutes.
• Melt chocolate chips in small saucepan
  over low heat, stirring constantly until
  smooth. Drizzle cookies with chocolate.
  Chill.   *Approximately 3½ dozen*

Prep time: 30 minutes plus chilling

◆ ◆ ◆

Pipe cream cheese into cookies using pastry tube with number 3 round tip.

STRAWBERRY COOL

1 (10 oz.) pkg. BIRDS EYE Quick
Thaw Strawberries in Syrup,
partially thawed
¼ cup whipping cream
1 (8 oz.) container PHILADELPHIA
BRAND Soft Cream Cheese with
Strawberries
1 cup coarsely crumbled pecan
shortbread cookies (approx.
8 cookies)

• Place strawberries and whipping cream in
  food processor or blender container;
  process until well blended.
• Blend in cream cheese.
• Alternately layer cookie crumbs and
  strawberry mixture in individual parfait or
  sherbet glasses. Chill. Top with additional
  whipped cream, if desired.
                              4 servings

Prep time: 10 minutes plus chilling

170

171

ALMOND PLUM TART

1 cup flour
¼ cup sugar
⅓ cup PARKAY Margarine
½ cup ground almonds
2 tablespoons cold water
1 (8 oz.) pkg. PHILADELPHIA
    BRAND Cream Cheese, softened
4 ozs. almond paste (approx. ½ cup)
2 tablespoons sugar
1 egg
½ teaspoon vanilla
1 (17 oz.) can whole purple plums in
    extra heavy syrup, undrained
1 tablespoon sugar
    Plum Sauce

- Preheat oven to 350°.
- Mix together flour and ¼ cup sugar in medium bowl. Cut in margarine until mixture resembles coarse crumbs. Stir in almonds. Add water; stir until dough forms ball. Press onto bottom and sides of 9-inch tart pan. Bake 10 minutes.
- Beat cream cheese, almond paste, 2 tablespoons sugar, egg and vanilla at medium speed with electric mixer until well blended. Pour into crust.
- Drain plums, reserving liquid for Plum Sauce. Remove pits from plums. Place plums and 1 tablespoon sugar in food processor or blender container; process until smooth. Spoon over cream cheese mixture. Cut through batter with knife several times for marble effect.
- Bake 25 minutes. Cool. Chill. Serve with Plum Sauce.   *12 servings*

PLUM SAUCE

2 teaspoons cornstarch
2 teaspoons sugar
    Reserved plum liquid

- Mix cornstarch and sugar in small saucepan until well blended. Gradually add plum liquid.
- Bring to boil over medium heat, stirring constantly. Boil 3 minutes or until clear and thickened, stirring constantly.

Prep time: 20 minutes plus chilling
Cooking time: 25 minutes

RASPBERRY CHOCOLATE FONDUE

½ cup KRAFT Red Raspberry Preserves
1 (8 oz.) container PHILADELPHIA
    BRAND Soft Cream Cheese
1 cup BAKER'S Semi-Sweet Real
    Chocolate Chips
2 tablespoons raspberry-flavored
    liqueur

- Heat preserves in small saucepan until softened; strain.
- Mix together preserves and cream cheese in small bowl until smooth.
- Melt chocolate chips with liqueur in medium saucepan over low heat, stirring until smooth.
- Gradually add cream cheese mixture, beating with wire whisk until smooth and thoroughly heated. Serve warm with cake cubes, banana slices or orange sections.
                        1⅓ cups

Prep time: 20 minutes

172

Almond Plum Tart

CHOCOLATE TRUFFLES

Packaged in decorative containers, Chocolate Truffles make a lovely hostess gift.

1 (8 oz.) pkg. PHILADELPHIA
  BRAND Cream Cheese, softened
3 cups powdered sugar
1 (12 oz.) pkg. BAKER'S Semi-Sweet
  Real Chocolate Chips, melted
1 tablespoon coffee-flavored liqueur
1 tablespoon orange-flavored liqueur
1 tablespoon almond-flavored liqueur
  Ground nuts
  Powdered sugar
  Cocoa

- Beat cream cheese in large mixing bowl at medium speed with electric mixer until smooth. Gradually add 3 cups powdered sugar, mixing until well blended. Add melted chocolate; mix well.
- Divide chocolate mixture into thirds. Add different flavor liqueur to each third; mix well. Chill several hours.
- Shape chocolate mixture into 1-inch balls; roll in nuts, sugar or cocoa. Chill.

5 dozen

Prep time: 20 minutes plus chilling

Microwave Tip: Microwave chocolate chips in medium bowl on HIGH 1 to 2 minutes or until chocolate begins to melt, stirring every minute. Stir until chocolate is completely melted.

NAPOLEONS

1 frozen ready-to-bake puff pastry
  sheet
1 (8 oz.) container PHILADELPHIA
  BRAND Soft Cream Cheese
¼ cup powdered sugar
¼ teaspoon almond extract
1 cup whipping cream, whipped
½ cup powdered sugar
1 tablespoon milk
1 (1 oz.) square BAKER'S Semi-Sweet
  Chocolate, melted

- Thaw puff pastry sheet according to package directions.
- Preheat oven to 400°.
- On lightly floured surface, roll pastry to 15×12-inch rectangle. Cut lengthwise into thirds.
- Place pastry strips on large ungreased cookie sheet; prick pastry generously with fork. Bake 8 to 10 minutes or until light golden brown.
- Stir together cream cheese, ¼ cup sugar and extract in medium bowl until well blended. Fold in whipped cream.
- Spread two pastry strips with cream cheese mixture; stack. Top with remaining pastry strip.
- Stir together ½ cup sugar and milk in small bowl until smooth. Spread over top pastry strip. Drizzle with melted chocolate. Chill. *10 servings*

Prep time: 20 minutes plus chilling
Cooking time: 10 minutes

Microwave Tip: Microwave chocolate in small bowl on HIGH 30 seconds to 1 minute or until chocolate begins to melt, stirring every 30 seconds. Stir until chocolate is completely melted.

174

BISCOTTI

Italian tradition calls for dunking these crisp cookies in wine or coffee.

1 (8 oz.) pkg. PHILADELPHIA
   BRAND Cream Cheese, softened
¾ cup PARKAY Margarine
¾ cup sugar
1 teaspoon vanilla
½ teaspoon anise extract
4 eggs
3¼ cups flour
1 teaspoon CALUMET Baking Powder
⅛ teaspoon salt
½ cup sliced almonds, toasted

- Preheat oven to 400°.
- Beat cream cheese, margarine, sugar, vanilla and extract in large mixing bowl at medium speed with electric mixer until well blended. Blend in eggs.
- Gradually add combined dry ingredients; mix well. Stir in almonds.
- On well-floured surface with floured hands, shape dough into three 12×1½-inch logs. Place logs, 2 inches apart, on greased and floured cookie sheet.
- Bake 15 to 20 minutes or until light golden brown. (Dough will spread and flatten slightly during baking.) Cool slightly.
- Diagonally cut each log into ¾-inch slices. Place on cookie sheet.
- Continue baking 5 to 10 minutes or until light golden brown. Cool on wire rack.

3 dozen

Prep time: 15 minutes
Cooking time: 30 minutes

Variation: Substitute almond or lemon extract for anise extract.

CHOCOLATE FRUIT CRÊPE

The chocolate crêpes can easily be made ahead of time. Layer each crêpe between sheets of waxed paper. Wrap securely in foil and freeze.

½ cup flour
⅓ cup sugar
2 tablespoons cocoa
½ cup skim milk
1 egg
1 tablespoon oil
½ teaspoon vanilla
1 (8 oz.) container PHILADELPHIA
   BRAND Soft Cream Cheese with
   Pineapple
2 cups cut-up assorted fresh fruit
¼ cup powdered sugar

- Blend flour, sugar, cocoa, milk, egg, oil and vanilla in medium bowl until smooth.
- Heat nonstick 8-inch skillet over medium heat. Pour 2 tablespoons batter into skillet. Spread batter with back of spoon into 4- to 5-inch circle.
- Cook 30 to 45 seconds or until bubbles appear on top and edges are dry; turn. Continue cooking 1 minute. Remove from skillet. Repeat with remaining batter. Cool.
- Spread each crêpe with 2 tablespoons cream cheese; top with ¼ cup fruit. Fold in half. Sprinkle with powdered sugar.

8 servings

Prep time: 20 minutes
Cooking time: 20 minutes

176

Chocolate Fruit Crêpe

GERMAN SWEET CHOCOLATE CREAM CHEESE BROWNIES

1 (4 oz.) pkg. BAKER'S GERMAN'S Sweet Chocolate
¼ cup PARKAY Margarine
¾ cup sugar
2 eggs, beaten
1 teaspoon vanilla
½ cup flour
½ cup chopped nuts
4 ozs. PHILADELPHIA BRAND Cream Cheese, softened
¼ cup sugar
1 egg
1 tablespoon flour

- Preheat oven to 350°.
- Microwave chocolate and margarine in large bowl on HIGH 2 minutes or until margarine is melted. Stir until chocolate is completely melted.
- Add ¾ cup sugar; mix well. Blend in two eggs and vanilla. Stir in ½ cup flour and nuts; mix well. Spread into greased 8-inch square baking pan.
- In small bowl, mix cream cheese and remaining sugar, egg and flour until well blended. Spoon over brownie mixture; cut through batter with knife several times for marble effect.
- Bake 35 to 40 minutes or until wooden pick inserted in center comes out almost clean. (*Do not overbake.*) Cool. Cut into squares.   *16 servings*

Prep time: 15 minutes
Cooking time: 40 minutes

Conventional: Melt chocolate and margarine in 2-quart saucepan over low heat; stir constantly just until melted. Remove from heat. Continue as directed.

HOLIDAY PEPPERMINT CANDIES

One batch of these creamy candies goes a long way. Give some as gifts and keep some to enjoy yourself.

4 ozs. PHILADELPHIA BRAND Cream Cheese, softened
1 tablespoon PARKAY Margarine
1 tablespoon light corn syrup
¼ teaspoon peppermint extract or few drops peppermint oil
4 cups powdered sugar
Green and red food coloring
Sifted powdered sugar
Green, red and white decorating icing (optional)

- Beat cream cheese, margarine, corn syrup and extract in large mixing bowl at medium speed with electric mixer until well blended. Gradually add 4 cups powdered sugar; mix well.
- Divide mixture into thirds. Knead few drops green food coloring into one third; repeat with red food coloring and second third. Wrap each third in plastic wrap.
- Working with one color mixture at a time, shape into ¾-inch balls. Place on waxed paper-lined cookie sheet. Flatten each ball with bottom of glass that has been lightly dipped in sugar.
- Repeat with remaining mixtures. Decorate with icing. Chill.   *5 dozen*

Prep time: 30 minutes plus chilling

178

Holiday Peppermint Candies

LAYERED FROZEN MOUSSE TORTE

For variety, substitute your favorite flavor premium ice cream for coffee ice cream.

1½ cups chocolate wafer crumbs
     (approx. 30 wafers)
  6 tablespoons PARKAY Margarine,
     melted
  2 tablespoons sugar
  2 tablespoons PARKAY Margarine
  2 tablespoons sugar
  1 cup chopped almonds
  ½ cup cold water
  ¾ cup sugar
  1 (8 oz.) pkg. PHILADELPHIA
     BRAND Cream Cheese, softened
  6 (1 oz.) squares BAKER'S Semi-Sweet
     Chocolate, melted
1½ cups whipping cream, whipped
  1 pt. premium coffee ice cream

- Preheat oven to 350°.
- Stir together crumbs, 6 tablespoons margarine and 2 tablespoons sugar in small bowl; press onto bottom and 2 inches up sides of 9-inch springform pan. Bake 10 minutes.
- Meanwhile, melt 2 tablespoons margarine in medium skillet over medium heat. Stir in 2 tablespoons sugar and almonds; cook 1 minute. Reduce heat to low; continue cooking almonds until golden brown, stirring constantly.
- Spread hot almond mixture over hot crust; press down lightly. Cool.
- Stir together water and ¾ cup sugar in small saucepan. Bring to boil; reduce heat to medium. Simmer 3 minutes.

- Beat cream cheese in large mixing bowl at medium speed with electric mixer until smooth. Gradually add sugar mixture, scraping bowl as needed. Blend in chocolate. Fold in whipped cream.
- Spread half of chocolate mixture over almond mixture. Refrigerate remaining chocolate mixture. Place springform pan in freezer 2 hours or until chocolate mixture is firm.
- Soften ice cream to spreading consistency. Spread over frozen chocolate layer; top with remaining chocolate mixture.
- Freeze several hours or overnight. Let stand at room temperature 10 to 15 minutes before serving. Garnish with whipped cream, chocolate lace and coffee beans, if desired. *10 to 12 servings*

Prep time: 40 minutes plus freezing

◆ ◆ ◆

To make chocolate lace garnish, see directions page 156.

180

181

BUTTERSCOTCH PEANUT BARS

These bars are sure to be a kid's favorite that adults will love, too!

    1 (8 oz.) pkg. PHILADELPHIA
        BRAND Cream Cheese, softened
    ½ cup packed brown sugar
    ½ cup granulated sugar
    ¼ cup PARKAY Margarine
    ½ cup milk
    1 egg
    2 teaspoons vanilla
    2¼ cups flour
    1 teaspoon CALUMET Baking Powder
    ¼ teaspoon salt
    1 cup chopped salted peanuts
    1 cup butterscotch morsels
        Butterscotch Frosting
    ½ cup chopped salted peanuts

- Preheat oven to 350°.
- Beat cream cheese, sugars and ¼ cup margarine in large mixing bowl at medium speed with electric mixer until well blended. Blend in milk, egg and vanilla.
- Add combined dry ingredients; mix well. Stir in 1 cup peanuts and butterscotch morsels. Spread into greased 15×10×1-inch jelly roll pan.
- Bake 20 to 25 minutes or until wooden pick inserted in center comes out clean. Spread with Butterscotch Frosting. Sprinkle with ½ cup peanuts. Cut into bars.   *Approximately 3 dozen*

BUTTERSCOTCH FROSTING

    1 cup butterscotch morsels
    ½ cup creamy peanut butter
    2 tablespoons PARKAY Margarine
    1 tablespoon milk

- Stir together all ingredients in small saucepan over low heat until smooth.

Prep time: 20 minutes
Cooking time: 25 minutes

CRANBERRY FOOL

Derived from the French word "fouler," which means to crush or press, a fool is generally a chilled dessert made of sweetened fruit pulp folded into a whipped cream mixture.

    1 (8 oz.) container PHILADELPHIA
        BRAND Soft Cream Cheese
    2 tablespoons orange juice
    1 tablespoon sugar
    1 (10 oz.) container frozen cranberry-
        orange sauce, thawed
    2 cups thawed COOL WHIP Whipped
        Topping

- Stir together cream cheese, orange juice and sugar in large bowl until well blended. Add sauce; mix well.
- Fold in whipped topping. Chill. Garnish with cranberries and mint leaves, if desired.   *4 servings*

Prep time: 10 minutes plus chilling

WHITE CHOCOLATE FUDGE

    1 (8 oz.) pkg. PHILADELPHIA
        BRAND Cream Cheese, softened
    4 cups powdered sugar
    1½ teaspoons vanilla
    12 ozs. white chocolate, melted
    ¾ cup chopped dried apricots
    ¾ cup chopped macadamia nuts

- Beat cream cheese, sugar and vanilla in large mixing bowl at medium speed with electric mixer until well blended. Gradually add chocolate; mix well. Stir in apricots and nuts.
- Spread into greased 8-inch square baking pan. Chill several hours. Cut into squares.   *2½ pounds*

Prep time: 15 minutes plus chilling

182

Cranberry Fool

CUSTARD BREAD PUDDING

2 (8 oz.) pkgs. PHILADELPHIA
    BRAND Cream Cheese, softened
½ cup packed brown sugar
1 teaspoon vanilla
1 teaspoon grated lemon peel
2½ cups milk
3 eggs, beaten
2 tablespoons whiskey or brandy
8 cups stale cinnamon-raisin bread
    cubes

- Beat cream cheese, sugar, vanilla and peel in large mixing bowl at medium speed with electric mixer until well blended. Gradually add milk, eggs and whiskey; mix well.
- Place bread in large bowl. Pour cream cheese mixture over bread; mix well. Let stand 30 minutes, stirring occasionally.
- Preheat oven to 325°.
- Pour mixture into greased 2-quart casserole; cover.
- Bake 40 minutes. Uncover; continue baking 35 minutes. Let stand at least 1 hour before serving. Serve with half and half or milk.   *10 to 12 servings*

Prep time: 10 minutes plus standing
Cooking time: 1 hour and 15 minutes

ALMOND AMARETTO DESSERT

1 (8 oz.) container Light
    PHILADELPHIA BRAND
    Pasteurized Process Cream Cheese
    Product
2 cups skim milk
1 (9 oz.) pkg. JELL-O Vanilla Flavor
    Sugar Free Instant Pudding and
    Pie Filling
3 tablespoons almond-flavored liqueur
1 (1.65 oz.) milk chocolate bar, grated
2 cups COOL WHIP Whipped Topping,
    thawed
⅓ cup sliced almonds, toasted

- Blend cream cheese product and ½ cup milk in large mixing bowl at low speed with electric mixer until well blended.
- Whisk together remaining milk with pudding mix in medium bowl until well blended. Add to cream cheese mixture; mix well. Stir in liqueur; pour into 1½-quart straight-sided glass bowl. Chill.
- Sprinkle half of grated chocolate over cream cheese mixture. Spoon whipped topping over chocolate. Sprinkle with almonds and remaining chocolate.
                              8 servings

Prep time: 30 minutes plus chilling

COFFEE TOFFEE PIE

2 cups chocolate wafer crumbs
    (approx. 40 wafers)
¼ cup sugar
6 tablespoons PARKAY Margarine,
    melted
1 (8 oz.) pkg. PHILADELPHIA
    BRAND Cream Cheese, softened
3 to 4 tablespoons coffee-flavored
    liqueur
1 (8 oz.) container COOL WHIP
    Whipped Topping, thawed
4 (1.4 ozs. each) milk chocolate-
    covered toffee bars, chopped
    (approx. 1 cup)

- Preheat oven to 350°.
- Stir together crumbs, sugar and margarine in medium bowl; press onto bottom and up sides of 9-inch pie plate. Bake 10 minutes.
- Beat cream cheese and liqueur in large mixing bowl at medium speed with electric mixer until well blended. Fold in whipped topping and ¾ cup candy; pour into crust.
- Sprinkle with remaining candy. Chill until firm.   *8 to 10 servings*

Prep time: 15 minutes plus chilling

184

Coffee Toffee Pie

FROZEN BANANA BOMBE

Be sure to remove dessert from freezer 30 minutes before serving.

- 1 (20 oz.) can crushed pineapple in unsweetened juice, undrained
- 1 (8 oz.) pkg. Light PHILADELPHIA BRAND Neufchatel Cheese, softened
- 3 bananas
- ¼ teaspoon ground nutmeg
- 1 cup vanilla ice milk
- 3 bananas, sliced
- ¼ cup BAKER'S ANGEL FLAKE Coconut, toasted

- Drain pineapple, reserving 3 tablespoons juice.
- Place neufchatel cheese, pineapple, reserved juice, three bananas and nutmeg in food processor or blender container; process until blended. Add ice milk; process until well blended.
- Fold in banana slices and coconut; pour into lightly oiled 8-cup mold or bowl. Freeze 4 to 6 hours or until firm.
- Remove from freezer 30 minutes before serving; unmold. Serve with KRAFT Hot Fudge Topping, if desired.   *8 servings*

Prep time: 30 minutes plus freezing and standing

STAR GAZER'S DIP

- 1 (8 oz.) container PHILADELPHIA BRAND Soft Cream Cheese with Pineapple
- 3 tablespoons orange juice
- 1 tablespoon powdered sugar
- 1 teaspoon grated orange peel

- Beat ingredients in small mixing bowl at medium speed with electric mixer until well blended. Chill. Serve with skewered assorted fresh fruit dippers. Garnish with orange peel, if desired.   *1 cup*

Prep time: 10 minutes plus chilling

CHOCOLATE–CHOCOLATE CAKE

- 1 (8 oz.) pkg. PHILADELPHIA BRAND Cream Cheese, softened
- 1 cup BREAKSTONE'S Sour Cream
- ½ cup coffee-flavored liqueur or cold water
- 2 eggs
- 1 two-layer chocolate cake mix
- 1 (4 oz.) pkg. JELL-O Chocolate Flavor Instant Pudding and Pie Filling
- 1 cup BAKER'S Semi-Sweet Real Chocolate Chips
- Sifted powdered sugar

- Preheat oven to 325°.
- Beat cream cheese in large mixing bowl at medium speed with electric mixer until smooth. Blend in sour cream, liqueur and eggs.
- Add cake mix and pudding mix; beat until well blended. Stir in chocolate chips.
- Pour into greased and floured 10-inch fluted tube pan.
- Bake 1 hour to 1 hour and 5 minutes or until wooden pick inserted near center comes out clean. Cool 5 minutes. Remove from pan. Cool completely. Sprinkle with powdered sugar just before serving.
      10 to 12 servings

Prep time: 10 minutes plus cooling
Cooking time: 1 hour and 5 minutes

Star Gazer's Dip

PHILLY MANDARIN DESSERT

    1 (1.3 oz.) pkg. DREAM WHIP
       Whipped Topping Mix
½ cup cold skim milk
    1 teaspoon vanilla
    1 (11 oz.) can mandarin orange
       segments, undrained
    1 (3 oz.) pkg. JELL-O Brand Orange
       Flavor Sugar Free Gelatin
½ cup cold water
    1 (8 oz.) pkg. Light PHILADELPHIA
       BRAND Neufchatel Cheese,
       softened
    1 (8 oz.) container exotic fruit- or
       lemon-flavored yogurt
½ cup BAKER'S ANGEL FLAKE
       Coconut, toasted

- Beat topping mix, milk and vanilla in small mixing bowl at high speed with electric mixer until soft peaks form. Chill.
- Drain orange segments, reserving syrup; pour syrup into small saucepan. Bring syrup to boil. Dissolve gelatin in syrup; add water. Chill until thickened but not set.
- Beat neufchatel cheese and yogurt in large mixing bowl at medium speed with electric mixer until well blended. Gradually add gelatin mixture. Chill 15 minutes.
- Fold orange segments and whipped topping into neufchatel cheese mixture. Spoon into individual serving dishes. Chill until firm. Sprinkle with coconut.

6 to 8 servings

Prep time: 25 minutes plus chilling

HOLIDAY CHARLOTTE RUSSE

For an elegant presentation, tie a colorful ribbon around this festive dessert.

  18 ladyfingers, split
    2 tablespoons rum (optional)
1½ teaspoons unflavored gelatin
    3 cups eggnog
    2 (8 oz.) pkgs. PHILADELPHIA
       BRAND Cream Cheese, softened
    2 (3½ oz.) pkgs. JELL-O Vanilla Flavor
       Instant Pudding and Pie Filling
    1 teaspoon rum extract
¼ teaspoon ground nutmeg
    1 cup whole berry cranberry sauce

- Place ladyfingers, cut sides in, on bottom and around sides of 9-inch springform pan; sprinkle with rum.
- Soften gelatin in ¼ cup eggnog in medium saucepan; stir over low heat 5 minutes or until dissolved. Stir in remaining 2¾ cups eggnog.
- Beat cream cheese in large mixing bowl at medium speed with electric mixer until smooth. Add eggnog mixture alternately with pudding mix, mixing well after each addition. Stir in extract and nutmeg.
- Pour into ladyfinger-lined springform pan. Chill 8 hours or overnight.
- Loosen ladyfingers from rim of pan; remove rim. Top with cranberry sauce just before serving. Garnish with ribbon, if desired. *10 to 12 servings*

Prep time: 15 minutes plus chilling

189

SUGARED CRÈME BRÛLÉE

The use of a water bath helps prevent the custard mixture from overcooking and curdling.

¼ cup PARKAY Margarine
½ cup packed brown sugar
1 tablespoon cold water
1 (8 oz.) pkg. PHILADELPHIA
    BRAND Cream Cheese, softened
⅓ cup packed brown sugar
2 teaspoons vanilla
6 eggs
2 cups half and half

• Preheat oven to 350°.
• Melt margarine in small saucepan. Stir in ½ cup sugar and water. Cook over medium heat 2 minutes or until well blended, stirring constantly. Spoon into eight (6-ounce) custard cups.
• Beat cream cheese, ⅓ cup sugar and vanilla in large mixing bowl at medium speed with electric mixer until well blended.
• Add eggs, one at a time, mixing well after each addition. Blend in half and half.
• Pour over sugar mixture in custard cups. Place cups in large shallow baking pan. Place baking pan on oven rack; carefully pour boiling water into baking pan to ½-inch depth.
• Bake 35 to 40 minutes or until center is set and knife inserted near centers comes out clean.
• Remove cups from water immediately; cool 5 minutes. Unmold onto serving plates.   *8 servings*

Prep time: 15 minutes
Cooking time: 40 minutes

CHEESECAKE MACAROON BARS

These bars are a great treat for afternoon tea, brunch or a casual party.

1 cup flour
1 cup ground almonds
½ cup PARKAY Margarine
⅓ cup packed brown sugar
¼ teaspoon salt
¼ teaspoon almond extract
2 (8 oz.) pkgs. PHILADELPHIA
    BRAND Cream Cheese, softened
¾ cup granulated sugar
1 tablespoon lemon juice
3 eggs
1 cup BAKER'S ANGEL FLAKE
    Coconut, toasted
1½ cups BREAKSTONE'S Sour Cream
3 tablespoons granulated sugar
2 teaspoons vanilla
½ cup BAKER'S ANGEL FLAKE
    Coconut, toasted

• Preheat oven to 350°.
• Beat flour, almonds, margarine, brown sugar, salt and extract in small mixing bowl at medium speed with electric mixer until well blended. Press onto bottom of 13×9-inch baking pan.
• Bake 8 to 10 minutes or until lightly browned.
• Beat cream cheese, ¾ cup granulated sugar and lemon juice in large mixing bowl at medium speed with electric mixer until well blended.
• Add eggs, one at a time, mixing well after each addition. Stir in 1 cup coconut; pour over crust.
• Bake 25 minutes. Cool 5 minutes.
• Stir together sour cream, 3 tablespoons granulated sugar and vanilla in small bowl until smooth; carefully spread over coconut mixture.
• Bake 5 to 7 minutes or until set. Sprinkle with ½ cup coconut; cool. Cut into bars.
Approximately 3 dozen

Prep time: 30 minutes plus cooling
Cooking time: 32 minutes

190

191

AMARETTO BREEZE

Easy elegance...for a refreshing change, serve the sauce with melon balls, raspberries, sliced peaches or a combination of these fruits.

>   1 (8 oz.) pkg. PHILADELPHIA
>   BRAND Cream Cheese, softened
>   ½ cup BREAKSTONE'S Sour Cream
>   ½ cup sugar
>   3 tablespoons almond-flavored liqueur
>   2 tablespoons whipping cream
>   1 pt. blackberries or blueberries
>   1 pt. strawberries

- Beat cream cheese and sour cream in small mixing bowl at medium speed with electric mixer until well blended. Blend in sugar, liqueur and cream. Chill.
- Place berries in individual serving dishes; top with cream cheese sauce.

4 to 6 servings

Prep time: 10 minutes plus chilling

MADISON AVENUE MOCHA BROWNIES

Very sophisticated...easy brownies made from a mix, but marbled with a mocha blend of coffee and sweetened cream cheese.

>   1 (20 to 23 oz.) pkg. brownie mix (plus
>   ingredients to prepare mix)
>   1 (8 oz.) pkg. PHILADELPHIA
>   BRAND Cream Cheese, softened
>   ⅓ cup sugar
>   1 egg
>   1½ teaspoons MAXWELL HOUSE
>   Instant Coffee Granules
>   1 teaspoon vanilla

- Preheat oven to 350°.
- Prepare brownie mix according to package directions. Pour into greased 13×9-inch baking pan.

- Beat cream cheese, sugar and egg in small mixing bowl at medium speed with electric mixer until well blended.
- Dissolve coffee in vanilla; add to cream cheese mixture, mixing until well blended.
- Spoon cream cheese mixture over brownie batter; cut through batter with knife several times for marble effect.
- Bake 35 to 40 minutes or until cream cheese mixture is set.   *4 dozen*

Prep time: 20 minutes
Cooking time: 40 minutes

SUNSHINE FRUIT TARTS

>   1 (15 oz.) pkg. refrigerated pie crusts
>   (2 crusts)
>   ⅓ cup KRAFT Pineapple Preserves
>   ⅓ cup KRAFT Strawberry Preserves
>   1 (8 oz.) container PHILADELPHIA
>   BRAND Soft Cream Cheese with
>   Pineapple
>   1 (8 oz.) container PHILADELPHIA
>   BRAND Soft Cream Cheese with
>   Strawberries

- Preheat oven to 450°.
- Roll each pie crust on lightly floured surface to 15-inch circle; cut each circle into eighteen circles with 3-inch cookie cutter. Place in miniature muffin pans or individual miniature tart pans; trim excess dough. Prick bottom and sides with fork.
- Bake 8 to 10 minutes or until lightly browned. Cool. Remove from pans.
- Spoon scant teaspoonful of preserves into each pastry shell; top with cream cheese.

3 dozen

Prep time: 35 minutes
Cooking time: 10 minutes

Tip: Pipe cream cheese into pastry shells using pastry tube with star tip.

192

Amaretto Breese

LEMON CHEESECAKE SQUARES

1⅓ cups shortbread cookie crumbs
  (approx. 18 cookies)
⅓ cup ground almonds
3 tablespoons PARKAY Margarine,
  melted
2 tablespoons sugar
1 (6 oz.) container frozen lemonade
  concentrate, thawed
3 (8 oz.) pkgs. PHILADELPHIA
  BRAND Cream Cheese, softened
1 cup BREAKSTONE'S Sour Cream
1 (3½ oz.) pkg. JELL-O Brand Lemon
  Flavor Instant Pudding and Pie
  Filling
2 cups thawed COOL WHIP Whipped
  Topping

- Preheat oven to 350°.
- Stir together crumbs, almonds, margarine and sugar in small bowl; press onto bottom of 13×9-inch baking pan. Bake 10 minutes. Cool.
- Gradually add lemonade concentrate to cream cheese in large mixing bowl, mixing at low speed with electric mixer until well blended. Add sour cream and pudding mix; beat 1 minute.
- Fold in whipped topping; pour over crust.
- Freeze until firm. Cut into squares.

18 servings

Prep time: 15 minutes plus freezing

CREAMY RASPBERRY DESSERT

Perfect for that special occasion!

1 envelope unflavored gelatin
¼ cup cold water
1 (8 oz.) pkg. Light PHILADELPHIA
  BRAND Neufchatel Cheese,
  softened
1 (15 oz.) container lowfat ricotta
  cheese
⅓ cup sugar or 6 packets sugar
  substitute
1 teaspoon vanilla
2 cups thawed COOL WHIP Whipped
  Topping
1 (10 oz.) pkg. BIRDS EYE Quick
  Thaw Red Raspberries in a Lite
  Syrup, thawed

- Soften gelatin in water in small saucepan; stir over low heat until dissolved.
- Beat cheeses, sugar and vanilla in large mixing bowl at medium speed with electric mixer until well blended. Gradually add gelatin, mixing until blended.
- Fold in whipped topping; pour into lightly oiled 4-cup mold. Chill until firm.
- Place raspberries in food processor or blender container; process until smooth. Strain. Unmold gelatin mixture; serve with purée. Garnish with fresh raspberries and fresh mint leaves, if desired.

8 servings

Prep time: 15 minutes plus chilling

194

195

PHILLY CREAM CHEESE COOKIE DOUGH

1 (8 oz.) pkg. PHILADELPHIA
    BRAND Cream Cheese, softened
¾ cup butter
1 cup powdered sugar
2¼ cups flour
½ teaspoon baking soda

- Beat cream cheese, butter and sugar in large mixing bowl at medium speed with electric mixer until well blended.
- Add flour and soda; mix well.

3 cups dough

Chocolate Mint Cutouts:

- Preheat oven to 325°.
- Add ¼ teaspoon mint extract and few drops green food coloring to 1½ cups Cookie Dough; mix well. Chill 30 minutes.
- On lightly floured surface, roll dough to ⅛-inch thickness; cut with assorted 3-inch cookie cutters. Place on ungreased cookie sheet.
- Bake 10 to 12 minutes or until edges begin to brown. Cool on wire rack.
- Melt ¼ cup mint-flavored semisweet chocolate chips in small saucepan over low heat, stirring until smooth. Drizzle over cookies.

Approximately 3 dozen

Prep time: 20 minutes plus chilling
Cooking time: 12 minutes per batch

Variation: Sprinkle cookies with nonpareils before baking.

Snowmen:

- Preheat oven to 325°.
- Add ¼ teaspoon vanilla to 1½ cups Cookie Dough; mix well. Chill 30 minutes.
- For each snowman, shape dough into two small balls, one slightly larger than the other. Place balls, slightly overlapping, on ungreased cookie sheet; flatten with bottom of glass. Repeat with remaining dough.
- Bake 18 to 20 minutes or until edges begin to brown. Cool on wire rack.
- Sprinkle each snowman with sifted powdered sugar. Decorate with icing as desired. Cut miniature peanut butter cups in half for hats.

Approximately 2 dozen

Prep time: 15 minutes plus chilling and decorating
Cooking time: 20 minutes per batch

Choco-Orange Slices:

- Preheat oven to 325°.
- Add 1½ teaspoons grated orange peel to 1½ cups Cookie Dough; mix well. Shape into 8×1½-inch log. Chill 30 minutes.
- Cut log into ¼-inch slices. Place on ungreased cookie sheet.
- Bake 15 to 18 minutes or until edges begin to brown. Cool on wire rack.
- Melt ⅓ cup BAKER'S Semi-Sweet Real Chocolate Chips with 1 tablespoon orange juice and 1 tablespoon orange-flavored liqueur in small saucepan over low heat, stirring until smooth. Dip cookies into chocolate mixture.

Approximately 2½ dozen

Prep time: 15 minutes plus chilling
Cooking time: 18 minutes per batch

Preserve Thumbprints:

- Preheat oven to 325°.
- Add ½ cup chopped pecans and ½ teaspoon vanilla to 1½ cups Cookie Dough; mix well. Chill 30 minutes.
- Shape dough into 1-inch balls. Place on ungreased cookie sheet. Indent centers; fill each with 1 teaspoon KRAFT Preserves.
- Bake 14 to 16 minutes or until edges begin to brown. Cool on wire rack.

3½ dozen

Prep time: 15 minutes plus chilling
Cooking time: 16 minutes per batch

Clockwise from top left: Preserve Thumbprints;
Snowmen; Choco-Orange Slices; Chocolate Mint Cutouts

PICNIC FRUIT TART

¾ cup flour
¼ cup oat bran
2 tablespoons sugar
¼ cup PARKAY Margarine
2 to 3 tablespoons cold water
1 envelope unflavored gelatin
½ cup cold water
1 (8 oz.) container Light
    PHILADELPHIA BRAND
    Pasteurized Process Cream Cheese
    Product
¼ cup sugar or 6 packets sugar
    substitute
1 teaspoon grated lemon peel
¼ cup skim milk
⅔ cup KRAFT Apricot Preserves
¾ cup grape halves
¾ cup plum slices

- Preheat oven to 350°.
- Mix together flour, oat bran and 2 tablespoons sugar in medium bowl; cut in margarine until mixture resembles coarse crumbs. Sprinkle with 2 to 3 tablespoons water, mixing lightly with fork until just moistened. Roll into ball. Cover; chill.
- Roll out dough to 11-inch circle on lightly floured surface. Place in 9-inch tart pan with removable bottom. Trim edges; prick bottom with fork.
- Bake 16 to 18 minutes or until golden brown; cool.
- Soften gelatin in ½ cup water in small saucepan; stir over low heat until dissolved. Cool.
- Beat cream cheese product, ¼ cup sugar and peel in large mixing bowl at medium speed with electric mixer until well blended. Gradually add gelatin and milk, mixing until well blended.

- Pour into crust. Chill until firm.
- Heat preserves in small saucepan over low heat until thinned. Spread evenly over tart. Arrange fruit over preserves. Carefully remove rim of pan.

14 servings

Prep time: 40 minutes plus chilling
Cooking time: 18 minutes

Variation: To make individual tarts, prepare dough as directed. Divide dough into fourteen equal portions; roll each into ball. Cover; chill. Roll each ball on lightly floured surface into 5-inch circle. Place in 3-inch tart pans; trim excess dough. Prick bottoms with fork. Bake 12 to 15 minutes or until lightly browned; cool. Continue as directed.

ALPINE STRAWBERRY BAVARIAN

1½ cups cold water
2 (3 oz.) pkgs. JELL-O Brand Lemon
    Flavor Sugar Free Gelatin
1½ cups cold water
1 (8 oz.) container Light
    PHILADELPHIA BRAND
    Pasteurized Process Cream Cheese
    Product
1 pt. strawberry ice milk or ice cream,
    softened
1 tablespoon lemon juice
2 cups strawberry slices

- Bring 1½ cups water to boil. Gradually add to gelatin in medium bowl; stir until dissolved. Stir in 1½ cups cold water.
- Gradually add gelatin to cream cheese product in large mixing bowl, mixing at medium speed with electric mixer until well blended.
- Stir in ice milk and lemon juice; fold in strawberries. Spoon into ten parfait glasses or 1½-quart bowl. Chill.

12 servings

Prep time: 20 minutes plus chilling

198

Picnic Fruit Tart

CHILLED LEMONADE DESSERT

1½ cups cold water
1 (3 oz.) pkg. JELL-O Brand Lemon
    Flavor Sugar Free Gelatin
1 (8 oz.) pkg. Light PHILADELPHIA
    BRAND Neufchatel Cheese,
    softened
⅓ cup frozen lemonade concentrate,
    thawed
1 teaspoon grated lemon peel
2 cups thawed COOL WHIP Whipped
    Topping

- Bring water to boil. Gradually add to gelatin in small bowl; stir until dissolved.
- Beat neufchatel cheese, lemonade concentrate and peel in large mixing bowl at medium speed with electric mixer until well blended. Stir in gelatin; chill until thickened but not set.
- Fold in whipped topping; pour into lightly oiled 6-cup mold. Chill until firm. Unmold. Garnish with peach slices, blueberries and fresh mint leaves, if desired.   *8 servings*

Prep time: 15 minutes plus chilling

Variation: Substitute eight individual ½-cup molds for 6-cup mold.

CHOCO–CHERRY BARS

1 (8 oz.) pkg. PHILADELPHIA
    BRAND Cream Cheese, softened
¾ cup PARKAY Margarine
1 cup sugar
2 eggs
1 teaspoon vanilla
1¼ cups flour
½ teaspoon baking soda
½ teaspoon salt
2 (1 oz.) squares BAKER'S
    Unsweetened Chocolate, melted
1 cup chopped maraschino cherries,
    well drained
½ cup chopped walnuts
    Chocolate Glaze

- Preheat oven to 350°.
- Beat cream cheese, margarine and sugar in large mixing bowl at medium speed with electric mixer until well blended. Blend in eggs and vanilla.
- Add combined dry ingredients; mix well.
- Blend in chocolate. Stir in cherries and walnuts.
- Spread into greased and floured 15×10×1-inch jelly roll pan.
- Bake 25 to 30 minutes or until wooden pick inserted in center comes out clean. Drizzle with Chocolate Glaze. Cut into bars.   *Approximately 3 dozen*

CHOCOLATE GLAZE

1 cup sifted powdered sugar
2 to 3 tablespoons milk
1 (1 oz.) square BAKER'S Unsweetened
    Chocolate, melted
½ teaspoon vanilla

- Mix together powdered sugar, milk, chocolate and vanilla until smooth.

Prep time: 25 minutes
Cooking time: 30 minutes

STRAWBERRY YOGURT ANGEL

1 (8 oz.) container PHILADELPHIA
    BRAND Soft Cream Cheese with
    Strawberries
½ cup vanilla yogurt
½ cup orange juice
1 tablespoon orange-flavored liqueur
    (optional)
1 (10-inch) tube angel food cake, sliced
1 pt. strawberries, sliced

- Place cream cheese, yogurt, orange juice and liqueur in food processor or blender container; process until smooth.
- Serve cream cheese sauce over cake slices; top with strawberries.
                    12 servings

Prep time: 10 minutes

201

Our Most Popular
Cheesecakes

PEANUT BUTTER CHOCOLATE CHEESECAKE

1 cup graham cracker crumbs
½ cup finely chopped peanuts
⅓ cup PARKAY Margarine, melted
2 tablespoons sugar
3 (8 oz.) pkgs. PHILADELPHIA
    BRAND Cream Cheese, softened
¾ cup sugar
2 tablespoons flour
1 teaspoon vanilla
3 eggs
5 (1.8 ozs. each) pkgs. milk chocolate
    peanut butter cups, chopped
    (approx. 1½ cups)
1 tablespoon flour

- Preheat oven to 325°.
- Mix together crumbs, peanuts, margarine and 2 tablespoons sugar in small bowl. Press onto bottom and 1½ inches up sides of 9-inch springform pan. Bake 10 minutes.
- Beat cream cheese, ¾ cup sugar, 2 tablespoons flour and vanilla in large mixing bowl at medium speed with electric mixer until well blended.
- Add eggs, one at a time, mixing well after each addition.
- Toss together chopped peanut butter cups with 1 tablespoon flour in small bowl. Stir into cream cheese mixture. Pour into crust.
- Bake 1 hour. Loosen cake from rim of pan; cool before removing rim of pan. Chill.

10 to 12 servings

Prep time: 20 minutes plus chilling
Cooking time: 1 hour

ALMOND CHEESECAKE WITH RASPBERRIES

This quick and easy dessert can be prepared in advance for elegant entertaining.

1¼ cups graham cracker crumbs
¼ cup PARKAY Margarine, melted
¼ cup sugar
2 (8 oz.) pkgs. PHILADELPHIA
    BRAND Cream Cheese, softened
1 (16 oz.) can ready-to-spread vanilla
    frosting
1 tablespoon lemon juice
1 tablespoon grated lemon peel
3 cups thawed COOL WHIP Whipped
    Topping
    Raspberries
    Sliced almonds

- Stir together crumbs, margarine and sugar in small bowl; press onto bottom and ½ inch up sides of 9-inch springform pan or pie plate. Chill.
- Beat cream cheese, frosting, juice and peel in large mixing bowl at medium speed with electric mixer until well blended.
- Fold in whipped topping; pour into crust. Chill until firm.
- Carefully remove rim of pan just before serving. Arrange raspberries and almonds on top of cheesecake. Garnish with fresh mint leaves, if desired.

10 to 12 servings

Prep time: 30 minutes plus chilling

203

SAVANNAH PEACH CHEESECAKE

Another great cheesecake using PHILLY Cream Cheese.

1 cup graham cracker crumbs
3 tablespoons PARKAY Margarine, melted
2 tablespoons sugar or 3 packets sugar substitute
1 envelope unflavored gelatin
½ cup cold water
1 (8 oz.) container Light PHILADELPHIA BRAND Pasteurized Process Cream Cheese Product
3 tablespoons sugar or 4 packets sugar substitute
⅛ teaspoon ground ginger
½ cup skim milk
2 (8 oz.) containers peach lowfat yogurt
2 fresh peaches, pitted, peeled, sliced
1 tablespoon lemon juice

- Stir together crumbs, margarine and 2 tablespoons sugar in small bowl; press onto bottom of 9-inch springform pan. Chill.
- Soften gelatin in water in small saucepan; stir over low heat until dissolved.
- Blend cream cheese product, 3 tablespoons sugar and ginger in large mixing bowl at medium speed with electric mixer until well blended. Gradually add gelatin and milk; mix well. Chill until mixture is thickened but not set.
- Fold in yogurt; pour over crust. Chill until firm.
- Carefully remove rim of pan just before serving. Toss together peach slices and lemon juice; drain. Arrange peaches on top of cheesecake. *8 servings*

Prep time: 30 minutes plus chilling

MARBLE CHEESECAKE SQUARES

1 cup flour
1 cup chopped hazelnuts
½ cup PARKAY Margarine
⅓ cup packed brown sugar
¼ teaspoon almond extract
3 (8 oz.) pkgs. PHILADELPHIA BRAND Cream Cheese, softened
¾ cup granulated sugar
1 tablespoon orange-flavored liqueur
1 teaspoon vanilla
3 eggs
1 (1 oz.) square BAKER'S Unsweetened Chocolate, melted

- Preheat oven to 325°.
- Beat flour, hazelnuts, margarine, brown sugar and extract in small mixing bowl at medium speed with electric mixer until well blended. Press onto bottom of 9-inch square baking pan. Bake 8 to 10 minutes or until lightly browned.
- Beat cream cheese, granulated sugar, liqueur and vanilla in large mixing bowl at medium speed with electric mixer until well blended.
- Add eggs, one at a time, mixing well after each addition.
- Blend melted chocolate into 1 cup batter; pour remaining batter over crust. Place chocolate batter in pastry tube. Pipe six strips on top of batter; cut through batter with knife several times for marble effect.
- Bake 30 to 35 minutes or until set. Chill. *15 servings*

Prep time: 15 minutes plus chilling
Cooking time: 35 minutes

◆ ◆ ◆

To soften cream cheese, microwave unwrapped packages in bowl on MEDIUM (50%) 30 seconds for each 8-ounce package.

204

Marble Cheesecake Squares

ALMOND BRICKLE CHEESECAKE

1 cup shortbread cookie crumbs
    (approx. 15 cookies)
3 tablespoons PARKAY Margarine,
    melted
1 tablespoon granulated sugar
3 (8 oz.) pkgs. PHILADELPHIA
    BRAND Cream Cheese, softened
⅔ cup granulated sugar
½ teaspoon vanilla
3 eggs
½ cup BREAKSTONE'S Sour Cream
1 (6 oz.) pkg. almond brickle chips
1 tablespoon flour
1 cup crushed shortbread cookies
    (approx. 13 cookies)
⅓ cup packed brown sugar
¼ cup PARKAY Margarine
1 cup chopped almonds
¼ cup KRAFT Caramel Topping

- Preheat oven to 350°.
- Mix together 1 cup crumbs, 3 tablespoons margarine and 1 tablespoon granulated sugar in small bowl. Press onto bottom of 9-inch springform pan. Bake 10 minutes.
- Beat cream cheese, ⅔ cup granulated sugar and vanilla in large mixing bowl at medium speed with electric mixer until well blended.
- Add eggs, one at a time, mixing well after each addition. Blend in sour cream.
- Toss together chips with flour in small bowl; stir into cream cheese mixture. Pour over crust.
- Mix together 1 cup crushed cookies and brown sugar; cut in ¼ cup margarine until mixture resembles coarse crumbs. Stir in almonds. Sprinkle over cream cheese mixture.
- Bake 1 hour and 5 minutes. Drizzle with caramel topping. Continue baking 10 minutes. Loosen cake from rim of pan; cool before removing rim of pan. Chill.

              10 to 12 servings

Prep time: 30 minutes plus chilling
Cooking time: 1 hour and 15 minutes

COOKIES 'N' CREAM CHEESECAKE

Everyone will love the cookies and cream combination—it's sure to be a hit!

1 cup chocolate sandwich cookie
    crumbs (approx. 12 cookies)
1 tablespoon PARKAY Margarine,
    melted
3 (8 oz.) pkgs. PHILADELPHIA
    BRAND Cream Cheese, softened
1 cup sugar
2 tablespoons flour
1 teaspoon vanilla
3 eggs
1 cup coarsely chopped chocolate
    sandwich cookies (approx.
    8 cookies)

- Preheat oven to 325°.
- Mix together crumbs and margarine in small bowl. Press onto bottom of 9-inch springform pan. Bake 10 minutes.
- Beat cream cheese, sugar, flour and vanilla in large mixing bowl at medium speed with electric mixer until well blended.
- Add eggs, one at a time, mixing well after each addition. Fold in chopped cookies. Pour over crust.
- Bake 1 hour and 5 minutes. Loosen cake from rim of pan; cool before removing rim of pan. Chill. Garnish with thawed COOL WHIP Whipped Topping, chocolate sandwich cookies, cut in half, and fresh mint leaves, if desired.

              10 to 12 servings

Prep time: 25 minutes plus chilling
Cooking time: 1 hour and 5 minutes

206

Cookies 'n' Cream Cheesecake

CHOCOLATE TRUFFLE CHEESECAKE

1 cup chocolate wafer crumbs (approx. 20 wafers)
3 tablespoons PARKAY Margarine, melted
2 (8 oz.) pkgs. PHILADELPHIA BRAND Cream Cheese, softened
⅔ cup sugar
2 eggs
1 cup BAKER'S Semi-Sweet Real Chocolate Chips, melted
½ teaspoon vanilla
Creamy Raspberry Sauce

- Preheat oven to 350°.
- Stir together crumbs and margarine in small bowl; press onto bottom of 9-inch springform pan. Bake 10 minutes.
- Beat cream cheese and sugar in large mixing bowl at medium speed with electric mixer until well blended.
- Add eggs, one at a time, mixing well after each addition.
- Blend in melted chocolate chips and vanilla; pour over crust.
- Bake 45 minutes. Loosen cake from rim of pan; cool before removing rim of pan. Chill.
- Spoon Creamy Raspberry Sauce onto each serving plate. Place slice of cheesecake over sauce. Garnish as desired. *10 to 12 servings*

CREAMY RASPBERRY SAUCE

1 (10 oz.) pkg. BIRDS EYE Quick Thaw Red Raspberries in a Lite Syrup, thawed
3 tablespoons whipping cream

- Place raspberries in food processor or blender container; process until smooth. Strain. Stir in cream.

Prep time: 30 minutes plus chilling
Cooking time: 45 minutes

A dusting of powdered sugar or cocoa is an attractive topping for bar cookies or cheesecakes. Place a paper doily or paper strips over the dessert. Sift powdered sugar onto the dessert just before serving. Carefully remove the doily or paper strips.

COFFEE MOCHA CRUNCH CHEESECAKE

This sophisticated cheesecake combines a crisp crust of chocolate wafers and nuts with a rich mocha cream cheese filling and a delicate coffee creme topping.

1¼ cups chocolate wafer crumbs (approx. 25 wafers)
⅓ cup PARKAY Margarine, melted
⅓ cup ground walnuts
¼ cup granulated sugar
1 (8 oz.) pkg. PHILADELPHIA BRAND Cream Cheese, softened
½ cup packed brown sugar
1 (1 oz.) square BAKER'S Unsweetened Chocolate, melted
2 teaspoons MAXWELL HOUSE Instant Coffee Granules
1 (16 oz.) container COOL WHIP Whipped Topping, thawed

- Stir together crumbs, margarine, walnuts and granulated sugar in small bowl; press onto bottom and up sides of 9-inch pie plate. Chill.
- Beat cream cheese, brown sugar, chocolate and coffee in large mixing bowl at medium speed with electric mixer until well blended.
- Fold in 3 cups whipped topping; pour over crust. Chill until firm.
- Top with remaining whipped topping.
8 servings

Prep time: 25 minutes plus chilling

Chocolate Truffle Cheesecake

RICE PUDDING CHEESECAKE

A new way to serve an old family favorite—as a cheesecake!

    1 cup graham cracker crumbs
    3 tablespoons sugar
    3 tablespoons PARKAY Margarine,
        melted
    4 (8 oz.) pkgs. PHILADELPHIA
        BRAND Cream Cheese, softened
    1 cup sugar
    1 tablespoon vanilla
    ½ teaspoon ground cinnamon
    4 eggs
1½ cups cooked MINUTE Rice
        Lingonberry Sauce

• Preheat oven to 350°.
• Mix together crumbs, 3 tablespoons sugar and margarine in small bowl. Press onto bottom of 9-inch springform pan. Bake 10 minutes.
• Beat cream cheese, 1 cup sugar, vanilla and cinnamon in large mixing bowl at medium speed with electric mixer until well blended.
• Add eggs, one at a time, mixing well after each addition. Stir in rice. Pour over crust.
• Bake 1 hour and 5 minutes. Loosen cake from rim of pan; cool before removing rim of pan. Chill. Serve with Lingonberry Sauce.   *10 to 12 servings*

LINGONBERRY SAUCE

    1 (14.11 oz.) jar lingonberries
    2 tablespoons cold water

• Place lingonberries in food processor or blender container; process until well blended. Strain. Stir in water.

Prep time: 35 minutes plus chilling
Cooking time: 1 hour and 5 minutes

MINI ALMOND CHEESECAKES

Have these on hand for those unexpected guests—these cheesecakes can be stored in the freezer up to one month.

    1 cup ground almonds
    2 tablespoons PARKAY Margarine,
        melted
    1 envelope unflavored gelatin
    ¼ cup cold water
    2 (8 oz.) containers Light
        PHILADELPHIA BRAND
        Pasteurized Process Cream Cheese
        Product
    ¾ cup skim milk
    ½ cup sugar or 12 packets sugar
        substitute
    ¼ teaspoon almond extract
    3 cups peeled peach slices

• Stir together almonds and margarine in small bowl. Press mixture evenly onto bottoms of twelve paper-lined baking cups.
• Soften gelatin in water in small saucepan; stir over low heat until dissolved.
• Beat cream cheese product, milk, sugar and extract in large mixing bowl at medium speed with electric mixer until well blended. Stir in gelatin. Pour into baking cups; freeze until firm.
• Place peaches in food processor or blender container; process until smooth. Spoon peach purée onto individual plates.
• Remove cheesecakes from freezer 10 minutes before serving. Peel off paper. Invert cheesecakes onto plates. Garnish with additional peach slices, raspberries and fresh mint leaves, if desired.
                              12 servings

Prep time: 20 minutes plus freezing and standing time

Note: For a sweeter peach purée, add sugar to taste.

211

CLASSIC CHEESECAKE

⅓ cup PARKAY Margarine
⅓ cup sugar
 1 egg
1¼ cups flour
 2 (8 oz.) pkgs. PHILADELPHIA
    BRAND Cream Cheese, softened
½ cup sugar
 1 tablespoon lemon juice
 1 teaspoon grated lemon peel
½ teaspoon vanilla
 3 eggs
 1 cup BREAKSTONE'S Sour Cream
 1 tablespoon sugar
 1 teaspoon vanilla

• Preheat oven to 450°.
• Beat margarine and ⅓ cup sugar in small mixing bowl at medium speed with electric mixer until light and fluffy; blend in one egg. Add flour; mix well.
• Spread dough onto bottom and 1½ inches up sides of 9-inch springform pan. Bake 5 minutes. Remove crust from oven. *Reduce oven temperature to 325°.*
• Beat cream cheese, ½ cup sugar, juice, peel and ½ teaspoon vanilla in large mixing bowl at medium speed with electric mixer until well blended.
• Add eggs, one at a time, mixing well after each addition; pour into crust.
• Bake at 325°, 50 minutes.
• Stir together sour cream, 1 tablespoon sugar and 1 teaspoon vanilla in small bowl. Spread evenly over cake; continue baking 10 minutes. Loosen cake from rim of pan; cool before removing rim of pan. Chill.
• Serve with BIRDS EYE Frozen Quick Thaw Strawberries in Syrup, thawed, if desired.   *10 to 12 servings*

Prep time: 30 minutes plus chilling
Cooking time: 1 hour

PEANUTTY HOT FUDGE CHEESECAKE

1½ cups graham cracker crumbs
 ⅓ cup PARKAY Margarine, melted
 ¼ cup granulated sugar
  1 (8 oz.) pkg. PHILADELPHIA
     BRAND Cream Cheese, softened
  1 cup powdered sugar
 ⅓ cup peanut butter
  3 cups thawed COOL WHIP Whipped Topping
 ¼ cup chopped peanuts
 ¼ cup KRAFT Hot Fudge Topping, heated

• Preheat oven to 350°.
• Stir together crumbs, margarine and granulated sugar in small bowl; press onto bottom and ½ inch up sides of 9-inch springform pan. Bake 10 minutes. Cool.
• Beat cream cheese, powdered sugar and peanut butter in large mixing bowl at medium speed with electric mixer until well blended.
• Fold in whipped topping; pour into crust. Sprinkle with peanuts. Chill until firm.
• Carefully remove rim of pan just before serving. Drizzle topping over cheesecake just before serving.   *10 to 12 servings*

Prep time: 15 minutes plus chilling

◆ ◆ ◆

You can determine that a cheesecake is done baking when the top has lost its sheen.

To lessen the effect of cracking, allow cheesecake to cool 5 minutes. Insert thin metal spatula between cake or crust and rim of pan; run spatula around inside edge to loosen cake.

212

Peanutty Hot Fudge Cheesecake

AMARETTO PEACH CHEESECAKE

3 tablespoons PARKAY Margarine
⅓ cup sugar
1 egg
¾ cup flour
3 (8 oz.) pkgs. PHILADELPHIA BRAND Cream Cheese, softened
¾ cup sugar
3 tablespoons flour
3 eggs
1 (16 oz.) can peach halves, drained, puréed
¼ cup almond-flavored liqueur

- Preheat oven to 450°.
- Beat margarine and ⅓ cup sugar in small bowl at medium speed with electric mixer until light and fluffy. Beat in one egg. Add ¾ cup flour; mix well.
- Spread dough onto bottom of 9-inch springform pan. Bake 10 minutes.
- Beat cream cheese, ¾ cup sugar and 3 tablespoons flour in large mixing bowl at medium speed with electric mixer until well blended.
- Add three eggs, one at a time, mixing well after each addition. Add peaches and liqueur; mix well. Pour over crust.
- Bake 10 minutes. *Reduce oven temperature to 250°.* Continue baking 1 hour and 5 minutes. Loosen cake from rim of pan; cool before removing rim of pan. Chill. *10 to 12 servings*

Prep time: 25 minutes plus chilling
Cooking time: 1 hour and 15 minutes

CARAMEL BROWNIE CHEESECAKE

1 (8 oz.) pkg. brownie mix
1 egg
1 tablespoon cold water
1 (14 oz.) bag KRAFT Caramels
1 (5 oz.) can evaporated milk
2 (8 oz.) pkgs. PHILADELPHIA BRAND Cream Cheese, softened
½ cup sugar
1 teaspoon vanilla
2 eggs
KRAFT Chocolate Topping

- Preheat oven to 350°.
- Mix together brownie mix, one egg and water in medium bowl until well blended. Spread into greased 9-inch square baking pan. Bake 25 minutes.
- Melt caramels with milk in heavy 1½-quart saucepan over low heat, stirring frequently until smooth. Reserve ⅓ cup caramel mixture for topping. Pour remaining caramel mixture over crust.
- Beat cream cheese, sugar and vanilla in large mixing bowl at medium speed with electric mixer until well blended.
- Add two eggs, one at a time, mixing well after each addition. Pour over caramel mixture in pan.
- Bake 40 minutes; cool. Chill.
- Heat reserved caramel mixture in small saucepan until warm. Spoon over individual servings of cheesecake; drizzle with chocolate topping.

12 to 16 servings

Prep time: 30 minutes plus chilling
Cooking time: 40 minutes

Variation: Substitute 9-inch springform pan for square baking pan. Loosen cake from rim of pan before cooling.

Microwave Tip: To melt caramels, microwave caramels with milk in small deep glass bowl on HIGH 2½ to 3½ minutes or until sauce is smooth when stirred, stirring after each minute.

214

215

Caramel Brownie Cheesecake

HOLIDAY EGGNOG CHEESECAKE

2 cups vanilla wafer crumbs (approx. 56 wafers)
6 tablespoons PARKAY Margarine, melted
1 teaspoon ground nutmeg
4 (8 oz.) pkgs. PHILADELPHIA BRAND Cream Cheese, softened
1 cup sugar
3 tablespoons flour
3 tablespoons rum
1 teaspoon vanilla
2 eggs
1 cup whipping cream
4 egg yolks

- Preheat oven to 325°.
- Mix together crumbs, margarine and nutmeg in small bowl. Press onto bottom and 1½ inches up sides of 9-inch springform pan. Bake 10 minutes.
- Beat cream cheese, sugar, flour, rum and vanilla in large mixing bowl at medium speed with electric mixer until well blended.
- Add two whole eggs, one at a time, mixing well after each addition. Blend in cream and yolks. Pour into crust.
- Bake 1 hour and 15 minutes. Loosen cake from rim of pan; cool before removing rim of pan. Chill. Sprinkle with additional ground nutmeg, if desired.

10 to 12 servings

Prep time: 20 minutes plus chilling
Cooking time: 1 hour and 15 minutes

CITRUS FRUIT CHEESECAKE

Assorted fresh fruit makes a festive topping for this traditional baked cheesecake with a hint of orange.

1 cup graham cracker crumbs
⅓ cup packed brown sugar
¼ cup PARKAY Margarine, melted
4 (8 oz.) pkgs. PHILADELPHIA BRAND Cream Cheese, softened
1 cup sugar
4 eggs
2 tablespoons grated orange peel
Assorted fresh fruit

- Preheat oven to 325°.
- Stir together crumbs, sugar and margarine in small bowl; press onto bottom of 9-inch springform pan. Bake 10 minutes.
- Beat cream cheese and sugar in large mixing bowl at medium speed with electric mixer until well blended.
- Add eggs, one at a time, mixing well after each addition. Blend in peel; pour over crust.
- Bake 50 minutes.
- Loosen cake from rim of pan; cool before removing rim of pan. Chill.
- Top with fruit. Garnish with lime zest, if desired.   *10 to 12 servings*

Prep time: 20 minutes plus chilling
Cooking time: 50 minutes

◆◆◆

Star fruit or carambola is a natural beauty. Its flavors range from slightly tart to sweet. Select firm, shiny fruit and allow to ripen at room temperature. Browning along the edges is a sign of ripening. Slice crosswise to form stars; do not peel.

216

Citrus Fruit Cheesecake

S'MORE CHEESECAKE

1¼ cups graham cracker crumbs
⅓ cup PARKAY Margarine, melted
¼ cup sugar
1 (12 oz.) container PHILADELPHIA
  BRAND Soft Cream Cheese
5 (1.45 ozs. each) milk chocolate candy
  bars, melted
1 (1.45 ozs. each) milk chocolate candy
  bar, finely chopped
1 cup KRAFT Miniature Marshmallows
1½ cups thawed COOL WHIP Whipped
  Topping

- Stir together crumbs, margarine and sugar
  in small bowl; press onto bottom and
  1 inch up sides of 9-inch springform pan.
- Stir together cream cheese and melted
  chocolate in small bowl until well blended;
  pour into crust. Sprinkle with chopped
  chocolate.
- Fold marshmallows into whipped topping;
  spread over cheesecake. Chill.

10 to 12 servings

Prep time: 15 minutes plus chilling

APPLESAUCE LEMON CHEESECAKE

1 cup gingersnap cookie crumbs
  (approx. 15 cookies)
¼ cup PARKAY Margarine, melted
3 (8 oz.) pkgs. PHILADELPHIA
  BRAND Cream Cheese, softened
⅔ cup sugar
3 tablespoons flour
3 eggs
1 cup applesauce
½ teaspoon grated lemon peel

- Preheat oven to 350°.
- Mix together crumbs and margarine in
  small bowl. Press onto bottom of 9-inch
  springform pan. Bake 10 minutes.
- Beat cream cheese, sugar and flour in
  large mixing bowl at medium speed with
  electric mixer until well blended.
- Add eggs, one at a time, mixing well after
  each addition. Blend in applesauce and
  peel. Pour over crust.
- Bake 1 hour and 15 minutes. Loosen cake
  from rim of pan; cool before removing rim
  of pan. Chill. *10 to 12 servings*

Prep time: 25 minutes plus chilling
Cooking time: 1 hour and 15 minutes

BANANA CHOCOLATE MINI CHEESECAKES

12 creme-filled chocolate cookies
1 (8 oz.) pkg. PHILADELPHIA
  BRAND Cream Cheese, softened
⅓ cup sugar
1 teaspoon lemon juice
2 eggs
½ cup mashed ripe banana
2 ozs. BAKER'S GERMAN'S Sweet
  Chocolate, broken into pieces
1½ tablespoons cold water
1½ tablespoons PARKAY Margarine
  Banana slices

- Preheat oven to 350°.
- Place one cookie onto bottom of each of
  twelve paper-lined muffin cups.
- Beat cream cheese, sugar and juice in
  large mixing bowl at medium speed with
  electric mixer until well blended.
- Add eggs, one at a time, mixing well after
  each addition. Blend in mashed banana;
  pour over cookies, filling each cup ¾ full.
- Bake 15 to 20 minutes or until set.
- Melt chocolate with water in small
  saucepan over low heat, stirring
  constantly. Remove from heat; stir in
  margarine until melted. Cool.
- Top cheesecakes with banana slices just
  before serving; drizzle with chocolate
  sauce. *12 servings*

Prep time: 15 minutes
Cooking time: 20 minutes

218

Index

INDEX